First World War
and Army of Occupation
War Diary
France, Belgium and Germany

47 DIVISION
Divisional Troops
238 Brigade Royal Field Artillery
1 March 1915 - 21 January 1917

WO95/2718/1

The Naval & Military Press Ltd
www.nmarchive.com
Published in association with The National Archives

Published by

The Naval & Military Press Ltd

Unit 10 Ridgewood Industrial Park,

Uckfield, East Sussex,

TN22 5QE England

Tel: +44 (0) 1825 749494

www.naval-military-press.com

www.nmarchive.com

This diary has been reprinted in facsimile from the original. Any imperfections are inevitably reproduced and the quality may fall short of modern type and cartographic standards.

© **Crown Copyright**
Images reproduced by permission of The National Archives, London, England, 2015.

Contents

Document type	Place/Title	Date From	Date To
Heading	WO95/2718 47 Div Mar 15-Jan 17 238 Brigade RFA		
Heading	1/8 London Bde Rfa Vol XIV		
Heading	47th Division 1-8th London (How) Bde Rfa Became 238th (How) Brigade R.F.A. Mar 1915-Jan 1917		
Miscellaneous	Subject		
Heading	8 London (How) Bde RFA 1915		
Heading	2nd London Division 8th London (How) Brigade RFA Vol I 1-31.3.15		
War Diary	Apsley	01/03/1915	15/03/1915
War Diary	Southampton	15/03/1915	15/03/1915
War Diary	Le Havre	16/03/1915	18/03/1915
War Diary	Berquette	19/03/1915	19/03/1915
War Diary	Ferfay	20/03/1915	31/03/1915
Heading	2nd London Division 8th London (How) Bde R.F.A. Vol II 1-30.4.15		
War Diary	Ferfay	01/04/1915	11/04/1915
War Diary	Le Touret	12/04/1915	30/04/1915
Heading	47th Division 8th London Bde R.F.A. Vol III 1-31.5.15		
War Diary	Le Touret	01/05/1915	25/05/1915
War Diary	La Motte	26/05/1915	28/05/1915
War Diary	Gorre	29/05/1915	31/05/1915
Heading	47th Division 8th London (How22) Bde RFA. Vol IV 1-30.6.15		
War Diary	Vermelles	01/06/1915	06/06/1915
War Diary	Ferfay	07/06/1915	24/06/1915
War Diary	Bois Des Dames	25/06/1915	30/06/1915
Heading	47th Division 1/8th London Bde RFA. Vol V 1-31-7-15		
War Diary	Bois Des Dames	01/07/1915	04/07/1915
War Diary	Gosnay	05/07/1915	10/07/1915
War Diary	Drouvin Wood	11/07/1915	11/07/1915
War Diary	Les Brebis	12/07/1915	29/07/1915
War Diary	Mont Evenic	30/07/1915	31/07/1915
Heading	47th Division 1/8th London Bde. R.F.A. Vol VI August 1 15		
War Diary	Mont Evenic Ref. Map. D.19.a 36 B,N.E. 1/20,000	01/08/1915	09/08/1915
War Diary	Mont Evenic	09/08/1915	31/08/1915
Heading	War Diary Headquarters 238th Brigade R.F.A. (1/8 London) (47th Division) September 1915		
War Diary	Drouvin Woods	01/09/1915	04/09/1915
War Diary	Les Brebis	05/09/1915	30/09/1915
Heading	47th Division 21st London Bty R.F.A. Sep 1915		
Heading	238th Brigade R.F.A. (1/8 London) 47th Division War Diary 21st London Battery R.F.A. September 1915		
War Diary		01/09/1915	30/09/1915
Heading	238th Bde. R.F.A. (1/8 London) 47th Div 22nd London Battery R.F.A. September 1915		
War Diary		01/09/1915	30/09/1915
Heading	47th Division 22nd London Bty R.F.A. Sep-Oct 1915		
War Diary	S. Maroc M2d.8.8	01/10/1915	31/10/1915
War Diary	Haillicourt	01/10/1915	03/10/1915

War Diary	Noeux-Les-Mines	04/10/1915	16/11/1915
War Diary	Ferfay	17/11/1915	30/11/1915
War Diary	Les Brebis	01/10/1915	31/10/1915
Heading	47th Division 1/8th London (How) Base R.F.A. Nov Vol IX		
War Diary	Les Brebis L.35.a.6.7 Sheet 36b.1/40,000	01/11/1915	04/11/1915
War Diary	Les Brebis	05/11/1915	15/11/1915
War Diary	Ferfay	17/11/1915	30/11/1915
War Diary	Les Brebis	30/11/1915	30/11/1915
War Diary	Frfay	30/11/1915	30/11/1915
Heading	1/8th (London) How Bde R.F.A. Dec Vol X		
War Diary	Ferfay B.18.b.2.3 Ref.map 36.b.1/40000	01/12/1915	11/12/1915
War Diary	Ferfay	11/12/1915	15/12/1915
War Diary	Noyelles L.11.d.3.0.	16/12/1915	18/12/1915
War Diary	Noyelles	19/12/1915	31/12/1915
Miscellaneous	A Form Messages And Signals		
Heading	8th London (Howitzer) Bde. R.F.A. (T.F.) 47th London Division IVth Corps		
Miscellaneous	File 8		
Heading	47th Divisional Artillery 238 8 London (How) Bde 1916		
Heading	8 London Bde (How) R.F.A. Jan Vol X		
War Diary	Noyelles-Les-Vermelles	01/01/1916	03/01/1916
War Diary	L.10.b.6.3.	04/01/1916	07/01/1916
War Diary	Grenay L.35.d.9.9.	08/01/1916	21/01/1916
War Diary	L.35.d.9.9.	22/01/1916	31/01/1916
Heading	1/8 London Bde R.F.A. Feb Vol XI		
War Diary	Grenay L.35.d.9.9.	01/02/1916	15/02/1916
War Diary	L.35.d.9.9.	16/02/1916	17/02/1916
War Diary	Ferfay	18/02/1916	19/02/1916
War Diary	Erny St. Julien	20/02/1916	21/02/1916
War Diary	Reclinghem and Dennebroeucq	22/02/1916	29/02/1916
Heading	1/8 London Bde Rfa Vol XIII		
War Diary	Reclinghem and Dennebroeucq	01/03/1916	11/03/1916
War Diary	Calonne Ricouart and Fosse De Clarence	12/03/1916	30/03/1916
Miscellaneous	M.G. R.A. 1st Army No. 0/39/9	06/03/1916	06/03/1916
War Diary	Frevillers	01/04/1916	30/04/1916
Miscellaneous	A Form Messages And Signals		
War Diary	Frevillers	01/05/1916	13/05/1916
War Diary	X.7.c.5.5.	14/05/1916	19/05/1916
War Diary	Frevillers	20/05/1916	23/05/1916
War Diary	Divion	26/05/1916	28/05/1916
War Diary	Barlin	29/05/1916	16/06/1916
War Diary	Boyeffles	16/06/1916	27/06/1916
Heading	47th Divisional Artillery 238th Brigade Royal Field Artillery July 1916		
War Diary	Boyeffles	01/07/1916	31/07/1916
Heading	47th Divisional Artillery 238th Brigade Royal Field Artillery August 1916		
War Diary	Conchy-Sur-Canche	01/08/1916	01/08/1916
War Diary	Outrebois	03/08/1916	05/08/1916
War Diary	Genne-Ivergny	06/08/1916	09/08/1916
War Diary	Lanches	10/08/1916	10/08/1916
War Diary	Wargnies	11/08/1916	11/08/1916
War Diary	Bavelincourt	12/08/1916	16/08/1916
War Diary	X.29.d.9.7.	17/08/1916	31/08/1916

War Diary	X.29.d.9.7. (Ref. Map 57d.S.E. 4	01/09/1916	22/09/1916
War Diary	S.21.a.1.1.	23/09/1916	30/09/1916
War Diary	S.21.a.1.1 (Ref. Map. 57 C.S.W. 1/20,000)	01/10/1916	13/10/1916
War Diary	Bavelincourt (Amiens 17 F. 1.)	14/10/1916	14/10/1916
War Diary	Talmas (Lens 11 D.6.)	16/10/1916	16/10/1916
War Diary	Authieule (Lens E.5)	17/10/1916	17/10/1916
War Diary	Conchy-Sur-Canche (Lens. C.3)	18/10/1916	18/10/1916
War Diary	Fontaine-Les-Boulans (Lens D.1.)	19/10/1916	19/10/1916
War Diary	Mametz (Hazebrouck 5a.d.5.)	20/10/1916	20/10/1916
War Diary	Watou (Hazebrouck 5a,H.2.)	21/10/1916	31/10/1916
War Diary	G.23.c.5.5 (Ref.map. 28.N.W. 1/20000)	04/11/1916	24/12/1916
War Diary	I.21.c.6.8 (Ref. Map 28 N.W. 1/20,000)	26/12/1916	29/12/1916
Heading	238 Bde RFA (8 London (How) Bde) January 1917		
Miscellaneous	Subject		
War Diary	I.21.c.6.8 (Ref.Map. 28.N.W. 1/20,000)	01/01/1917	21/01/1917

WO95/2718 (1)
47 Div
Mar '15 - Jan '17
238 Brigade RFA

47

1/8 London Bde
R.F.A.

Vol XIV

47TH DIVISION

1-8TH LONDON(HOW)BDE RFA
BECAME
238TH (HOW) BRIGADE R.F.A.
MAR 1915-JAN 1917

BDE BROKEN UP

Index................

SUBJECT.

Press 52
Drawer 1

$\frac{3}{}$

No.	Contents.	Date.

Austro-German Order of Battle Maps (Russian Front), 1918.

2 Jany. — 13 March 1918

Compiled in M.I. (W.O.)

FILE 9

HISTORICAL SECTION
MILITARY BRANCH.

1915 (Vol. I.)
YPRES, 1915

Sketch 14 _ Battle of St Julien, 26th April

(Corrected 1st Proof)

Instructions enclosed

8 London (How) Bde RFA

~~August~~ 1915

121/4872

2nd London Division

8th London (Hows) Brigade RFA.

Vol I. 1 — 31.3.15

Army Form C. 2118.

WAR DIARY
or
INTELLIGENCE SUMMARY.
(Erase heading not required.)

Instructions regarding War Diaries and Intelligence Summaries are contained in F. S. Regs., Part II. and the Staff Manual respectively. Title pages will be prepared in manuscript.

Place	Date	Hour	Summary of Events and Information	Remarks and references to Appendices
APSLEY	MARCH 1st	1915	LECTURE (Officers only) by MAJOR E.ETON 21st Co. London Battery. Experiences with Expeditionary Force	
	2nd		LECTURE (all ranks) by MAJOR E.ETON 21st Co. of London Battery - do. -	
	3rd		HORSE INSPECTION - Major Hamboro. D.A.D.R. 71 Horses Cast Medical Inspection all ranks.	
	4th		HARNESS INSPECTION	
	5th		Remounts received	
	6th		Remounts received	
	7th		Inspection by Inspector of Ordnance Machinery.	
	to		Preparations for Move Overseas. Obtaining Remounts, new Harness, Stores and Equipment.	
	14th		Orders received.	
	15th		All Documents required for Records of the Brigade packed and forwarded to Headquarters, of the Brigade for safe custody. All Billets paid up and all outstanding matters cleared up as far as possible, and every thing not to be taken away handed over to Officer in Charge Details left at War Station. (Capt. Mc.Veagh 2/8th London (How) Brigade R.F.A.) Brigade Entrained at WATFORD Station, travelling in 4 Trains and proceeded to SOUTHAMPTON. the last train reaching SOUTHAMPTON at 11.30 a.m.	
SOUTHAMPTON			Unfit Horses were replaced by Serviceable ones. The Brigade then embarked in different Transports, Headquarters with detachments from 21st Battery, 22nd Battery and Ammunition in S.S. Angle Canadian, sailing at 6.30 p.m. Remainder sailing in S.S.Chybassia and one other Transport.	

1577 Wt.W10791/1773 500,000 1/15 D. D. & L. A.D.S.S./Forms/C. 2118.

Army Form C. 2118.

WAR DIARY
or
INTELLIGENCE SUMMARY.
(Erase heading not required.)

Place	Date	Hour	Summary of Events and Information	Remarks and references to Appendices
Le HAVRE.	March 16		The Brigade arrived at Le Havre and disembarked. During disembarkation a small amount of Gear, such as Nosebags, and Head ropes were lost by the 21st Battery.	
			Warm clothing for men, Horse rugs and Stores to complete establishment were drawn from Ordnance Depot.	
			It was found necessary to unload the Wagons owing to tonnage of cranes not being sufficient to lift them loaded. Three Mark II Ammunition Wagons of the 21st Battery were injured by Slings of Cranes, footboards and Armoured Shield being torn off.	
			The Brigade then proceeded to No. 2 Rest Camp HAVRE, arriving 8.30 p.m.	
	17		The 21st Co. of London Battery proceeded to Gare des Merchandises HAVRE and entrained at 8.30 a.m.	
			M. Delpon Vissic – Interpreter joined the Brigade. Base Details & Orderly Room Sergeant left for HARFLEUR.	
			The remainder of the Brigade then proceeded to Gare des Merchandises HAVRE and entrained Headquarters and 22nd Co. of London Battery at 4 p.m. Ammunition Column at 7 p.m.	
	18		Brigade arrived at BERQUETTE travelling via MONTEROLIER BOCHY, ABBEVILLE, and ST.OMER. Instructions were received at ST.OMER to proceed on to BERQUETTE.	
BERQUETTE	19		Detrained and Marched to FERFAY, the billeting area for the Brigade as instructed by C.R.A. Interpreter and one Officer proceeded in advance to prepare Billets.	
			Route to FERFAY, through LILLERS.	

Army Form C. 2118.

WAR DIARY
or
INTELLIGENCE SUMMARY.
(Erase heading not required.)

Instructions regarding War Diaries and Intelligence Summaries are contained in F. S. Regs., Part II. and the Staff Manual respectively. Title pages will be prepared in manuscript.

Place	Date	Hour	Summary of Events and Information	Remarks and references to Appendices
FERFAY	March 20		Training continued GUN LAYING. GUN DRILL, DRIVING DRILL, and Practice with BUZZER for Telephonists.	
	21		Training as above.	
	22		Inspection by General Sir John FRENCH.	
	23		Training as above.	
	24		do.	
	25		do. 2 Officers, 2 N.C.O.s and 2 Telephonists attached to 1st Divisional Artillery for Instruction.	
			4 Officers, 4 N.C.O.s and 4 Telephonists attached to 2nd Divisional Artillery for course of Instruction.	
	26		Usual Training. Information received from G.O.C. R.A. 2nd London Division that 21st Battery would be temporarily attached to MEERUT Divn. Indian Corps. O.C. Major E.ETON to report personally on 1st April to G.R.A. MEERUT DIVN.	
	27		Usual Training.	
	28		Orders received by Major Eton O.C. 21st Battery to report to Brig.Genl. Johnson G.R.A. LAHORE Divn. on 30th March instead of 1st April at MEERUT divn.	
	29		2 Officers, 2 N.C.O.s and 22 Telephonists attached to 1st Divisional Artillery. 2 Officers, 2 N.C.O.s and 2 Telephonists attached to 2nd Divisional Artillery.	
			First parties returned to Brigade.	
			Orders received by Major Eton O.C. 21st Battery to report to General Johnson	

Army Form C. 2118.

WAR DIARY
or
INTELLIGENCE SUMMARY.
(Erase heading not required.)

Instructions regarding War Diaries and Intelligence Summaries are contained in F.S. Regs., Part II and the Staff Manual respectively. Title pages will be prepared in manuscript.

Place	Date	Hour	Summary of Events and Information	Remarks and references to Appendices
	MARCH			
FERFAY	29th contd		at REIZ BAILLEUL AT once. Major Eton reported accordingly. Instructions received that 21st Battery would come under orders temporarily of the C.R.A. Lahore Division., and would take part in a contemplated operation. Details as to the objectives:- consisting of 4 groups of Buildings received. Verbal orders to bring the Battery into position at about 7.p.m. on the 31st March 1915. Major Eton remained at REIZ BAILLEUL.	
	30th		O.C. 21st Battery (Major Eton) accompanied by Brigade Major R.A. LAHORE DIVISION reconnoitred position for Battery. In default of any more satisfactory position being available Major Eton decided to place Battery at Map 36 M.27 d. 7-5. Telephone wire and 2 Telephones were indented for. O.C. 21st Battery visited the D.A.D.O.S. and explained need for 7000 yards more Telephone wire. Purchased 2 wheeled cart, transport for baggage allowed according to Mobilization Store Table (G.1098-15) not being adequate. Then returned to FERFAY. Orders to move Battery to LAHORE DIVN cancelled.	
			Officer Commanding Brigade and Adjutant, together with O.C. 22nd Battery and 1 Subaltern proceeded Headquarters 2nd Divisional Artillery, reporting to G.O.C. and received orders to proceed to LE QUESNOY and report to O.C. 44th Brigade R.F.A. Commanding Officer, and Adjutant were attached to Headquarters 44th Bde., and Major Pollard (O.C. 22nd Battery) and Lieut. Kindell were directed to report to O.C. 47th Battery R.F.A.	X
	31st		Position required to be taken up by the 22nd Battery detailed and explained by the O.C. 44th Bde. R.F.A.. Orders received at 9 p.m. for the Officers of the 8th London (How) attached to the 44th Brigade to return to their Billeting area. Lt.Col. R.F.A. T.F. Officer Commanding 8th London (How) Brigade R.F.A.	

12/5256

2nd London Division

8th London (How'r) Bde R.F.A.

Vol II 1 — 30.4.15

Army Form C. 2118.

WAR DIARY
or
INTELLIGENCE SUMMARY.
(Erase heading not required.)

8th London (How.) Bde R.F.A.

Place	Date	Hour	Summary of Events and Information	Remarks and references to Appendices
FERFAY	April 1st		O.C. 22nd Battery, Capt. Largen, Lt. Kindell returned to Ferfay from attachment to 44th Btty. Batteries carry out Gun drill, Laying, Driving and Signallers practiced on buzzer.	
	2nd		Trainings as above.	
	3rd		Training as above	
	4th		Training as above.	
	5th		All N.C.O.s and Men were marched into AUCHEL in relays for bathing Parade at Auchel Mines.	
	6th		Inspection of 22nd Battery in Gun Drill, Laying, Signalling and Registration of Targets. 21st Battery and Ammunition Column carry out usual training.	
	7th		Usual Brigade training. 2 Telephonists from Brigade Headquarters and 2 from each Battery attached to 2nd London Divisional Artillery.	
	8th		Inspection of Batteries and Ammunition Column in Field Service Marching Order. Every vehicle, man and horse on parade. Turn out good.	
	9th		Officers Commanding 21st and 22nd batteries with Captains and 45 N.C.O.s and men from each battery (including all Telephonists) forwarded by Motor Busses, taking with them all entrenching tools and telephones, to BETHUNE from where they marched to Le Touret reporting to O.C. 25th Brigade R.F.A. (Lt.Col. Elton) at 2 P.M. Positions selected by Battery Commanders near Le Touret. Billets allotted for Batteries and Headquarters. Adjutant of Brigade followed reporting to G.O.C.Commanding 1st Divisional Artillery.	
	10th		Usual training for detachment left at Ferfay. Officers, N.C.O.s and Gunners at Le Touret continue preparations of Gun Emplacements.	

Army Form C. 2118.

WAR DIARY
or
INTELLIGENCE SUMMARY.
(Erase heading not required.)

Instructions regarding War Diaries and Intelligence Summaries are contained in F. S. Regs., Part II. and the Staff Manual respectively. Title pages will be prepared in manuscript.

Place	Date	Hour	Summary of Events and Information	Remarks and references to Appendices
FERFAY	April 11		Brigade complete (less the Officers and 45 N.C.O.s and men per Battery) moves at 8.45a.m. via AUCHEL,CHOQUES, to GONNEHEM.There Ammunition Column with Battery First Line Wagons march to BELLE RIVE and went into billets. 4 Gun Limbers of 21st Battery and 4 Firing Battery Wagons of 22nd Battery return same night from Firing line. Batteries placed guns in position at 8 p.m.	
LE TOURET	12		Batteries allotted Targets and receive instructions to register - 4 rounds per day being allotted. Observations Stations of Batteries selected to engage objectives allotted. Observation Station of 21st Battery - staging in roof of ruined farm 100 yards behind infantry firing line known as DEAD COW FARM (Map reference sheet 36 1/40,000 s 14 b 6.3). Observation Station of 22nd Battery s 14 b 9-6. Commence registration of Targets. Ammunition Column and all horses at wagon line 3 hours walking exercise.	
	13		Batteries continue registration.22nd Battery register 4 guns on WHITE HOUSE S 16 c 8.2. Officers of each Battery detailed to remain at Observation Station at all times, and 4 men with guns and 1 Officer at the Battery end.	
	14		Batteries carry improvement of gun-platforms, dug-outs etc.,	
	15		Batteries continue registration of Targets. 22nd Battery registers 2 guns on REDOUBT S 15 b 10.0. Shell burst at muzzle of No.2 Gun of the 22nd Battery resulting in seven casualties viz. Sgt.Johnson, Corpl. Moody, Bom.Saunders, a/Bom Honey, Gr,Orton, Gr,Britnell, wounded. Gunner Bishop killed.Board of enquiry held President Major E.Eton R.F.A. Two German high explosive shells burst within 100 yards of 21st Battery, pieces of shell fell around the Battery without casualties. Ammunition Column and Wagon Line of Batteries left BELLE RIVE at 3.45 p.m. travelling via HINGES and LOGON to LES GAUDRONS and again going into billets.	T.F.
	16		Batteries continue registration. N.C.O.s and Men sent from Wagon Line to replace casualties of yesterday.Brigade inspected by Brig.Gen.Wray. Ammunition Column supply 48 rounds of ammunition to Batteries.	

Army Form C. 2118.

WAR DIARY
or
INTELLIGENCE SUMMARY.
(*Erase heading not required.*)

Instructions regarding War Diaries and Intelligence Summaries are contained in F. S. Regs, Part II. and the Staff Manual respectively. Title pages will be prepared in manuscript.

Place	Date	Hour	Summary of Events and Information	Remarks and references to Appendices
LE TOURET	17		Registration continued. 21st Battery re-registered on SCHOOL HOUSE S 22 a 1.7. Two shells burst close behind German Breastwork. Fired one round on Rifle Battery S21 a 7.8. One abnormal round fell inside British lines without causing damage or casualty. Ammunition Column received 48 rounds of Ammunition from Divisional Ammunition Section at 12 noon. 32 rounds sent from Ammunition Column to Batteries at 6p.m. 32 rounds of Ammunition received from Divisional Ammunition Column 9p.m. 21st Gun limbers (filled) and 22nd Battery firing Wagons (empty) sent from Ammunition Column to firing line 1.30 a.m. Horses return to Wagon Line.	
	18		Registration continued. 21st Battery fired 2 rounds on Rifle Battery S 31 a 8.9 at 3.40 p.m. Target not registered. 22nd battery fired 8 rounds on CROSS ROADS S 16 d 1.4. A house near CROSS ROADS was seen to burst into flames a few minutes after 22nd Battery had ceased firing.	
	19		Registration continued. At 2.30 p.m. 22nd Battery fired 8 rounds against farm DE TOULOTTE S 22 b 4.9. 3.55p.m. 21st Battery fired 8 rounds registering one gun on HOUSES S 22 a 3.3 The last round of 21st Battery set fire to material behind one house. Ammunition Column driving drill.	
	20		Registration continued. 22nd Batteries fired 3 rounds against FARM DE TOULOTTE S 16 d 5.1 21st Battery did not fire - Stand fast being received. German Observation balloon up. 22nd Battery commence preparing new position for Battery.	
	21		Registration continued at 12.45 p.m. 21st Battery fired 9 rounds on HOUSE S 21 b 3.5 Two rounds did not explode. One round demolished part of the East of House. At 3.15 p.m. 13 rounds were fired on FME DE TOULOTTE S 16 d 5.1. O.C. 22nd Battery continued preparing new position.	
	22		Registration continued. by 22nd Battery At 4.16 p.m. 21st Battery fired 8 rounds at HOUSE S 21 b 2.5. One direct hit, second gun registered on Target. 4.30 p.m. 22nd Battery fired 8 rounds against enemy's redoubt S 15 b 9.8.	
	23		Registration continued by O.C. 22nd Battery. At 2.30 p.m. 22nd Battery fired 8 rounds against FME DE TOULOTTE. 21st B.ttery did not fire, registration having been completed. Shells from	

Army Form C. 2118.

WAR DIARY
or
INTELLIGENCE SUMMARY.
(Erase heading not required.)

Place	Date	Hour	Summary of Events and Information	Remarks and references to Appendices
LE TOURET	23		German Field Howitzers dropped near Battery. of 5 consecutive rounds, 2 failed to explode. 84 rounds of Ammunition received by Ammunition Column from Divisional Ammunition Column. 21st Battery limbers returned to Wagon line.	
	24		Registration of Batteries continued. At 3.30 p.m. 22nd Battery fire d 7 rounds against enemy's trenches s 15 b 2.3. At 3.55 p.m. 21st Battery fired 9 rounds at German Breastwork s 15 d 6.2 Two rounds burst X just over and blew a quantity of the back of the Breastwork away. The firing was the most consistent yet experienced.	
	25		Batteries did not fire as registration of allotted Targets was completed. Repair of guns, platforms and emplacements. O.C. inspects Wagon Line, all horses and vehicles examined. Church Parade.	
	26		Nothing to report. Batteries practice laying out of night line. Map reading, and repair and overhaul of all wires. Arrangements for baths for the men. Each Battery and Headquarters can have a bath at least once during the week. New dug-outs built.	
	27		Batteries continue to carry out inspection of all stores and equipment. Map reading, laying etc. Stores not required by Batteries sent to Wagon line i.e. plugs, fuze caps, tubes (expended) cartridge covers etc.	
	28		Batteries continue registration on Targets. 21st Battery at 5.12 p.m. fired 7 rounds on 1 s 16 c 8.8 22nd Battery fired 9 rounds on 4 S 22 a 2.7 and 3 rounds on 10 s 22 a 3.3. Germans shell breastwork of ours between 4 and 5 p.m. Debris was thrown onto Observation Station (DEAD COW FARM) but without damage. Both the 21st Battery telephone wires were cut.	
	29		Registration continued on Targets. 21st Battery fired 2 rounds on Target 7 s 1 6 d 3.1 and registered. At 4.6 p.m. fired 9 rounds and registered on Targets 2 S 16 d 1.3 and 11 s 15 b 2.3 and at 12.30 p.m. 22nd Battery fired 11 rounds on Target 3 s 15 d 6.2 and registered. At 4.30 p.m. the 22nd battery fired 9 rounds on Target 9 S 21 b 3.5 and registered.	

Army Form C. 2118.

WAR DIARY
or
INTELLIGENCE SUMMARY.
(Erase heading not required.)

Instructions regarding War Diaries and Intelligence Summaries are contained in F. S. Regs., Part II. and the Staff Manual respectively. Title pages will be prepared in manuscript.

Place	Date	Hour	Summary of Events and Information	Remarks and references to Appendices
LE TOURET	30		At 11.5 p.m. 21st Battery fired 4 rounds on night lines. Targets 3- s 22 a 2.7 6- S 21 c 3.5 9- S 21 b 3.5 10- S 22 a 3.3	
			At 11.5 p.m. 22nd Battery fired 4 rounds on night lines. Targets 1- s 16 c 8.8 2- s 16 d 1.5 7- s 16 d 3.1 8- S 15 b 9.8.	

Lt. Col. R.F.A. T.F.
Officer Commanding
8th London (How) R.A. Brigade.

121/5576

High Division

5th London Bde R.F.A.

Vol III   1 — 31.5.15

Army Form C. 2118.

WAR DIARY
or
INTELLIGENCE SUMMARY.
(Erase heading not required.)

Instructions regarding War Diaries and Intelligence Summaries are contained in F.S. Regs., Part II. and the Staff Manual respectively. Title pages will be prepared in manuscript.

Place	Date	Hour	Summary of Events and Information	Remarks and references to Appendices
LE TOURET	May 1st		Attached to 1st Division; grouped with 25th Brigade. 22nd Battery fired 4 rounds registering targets on the RICHEBOURG - FESTUBERT front. Ammunition circuit reconnoitred. 8 men attached to Batteries from Ammunition Column for instruction, and replaced by 8 from Batteries. Ammunition Column issued 86 rounds to Batteris and received same from Divisional Ammunition Column.	
	2		Batteries did not fire. Improved gun platforms.	
	3		Batteries did not fire. Improved gun platforms.	
	4		Batteries registered new targets on the FESTUBERT front. A large proportion of German Shell was observed not to burst. Major Popham R.F.A. Adjutant, transferred to 1st Divisional Artillery and Lt. E.R.Cooper appointed Adjutant.	
	5		22nd Battery fired 8 rounds on enemy's breastworks. 21st Battery improved their gun platforms etc.	
	6		Batteries did not fire. Ammunition Column received 208 rounds from Divisional Ammunition Column.	
	7		Batteries registered on German trenches and breastworks on FESTUBERT front. Ammunition and Wagon lines received orders to be ready to move by 6 a.m. 8/5/15. Orders to "Stand fast" received at 9 p.m.	
	8		Attached to 2nd Division and grouped with 44th Brigade. Additional German trenches registered. Germans seen in FERME DU BOIS. RICHEBOURG. One N.C.O and a man slightly wounded by accidentally dropping an unexploded German fuse. 3 H.D. and 5 D remounts taken on strength of Ammunition Column. Orders given to Ammunition Column to be ready to move by 6 a.m. 9/5/15.	
	9	5.10am.	Batteries took part in bombardment of German trenches preparatory to Infantry attack on the RICHEBOURG - FESTUBERT line.	
		4.30pm	ceased bombardment. Wagon line paraded ready to move at 5 a.m. Ammunition Column issued 776 rounds to Batteries and received same from Divisional Ammunition Column.	

Army Form C. 2118.

WAR DIARY
or
INTELLIGENCE SUMMARY.

(Erase heading not required.)

Instructions regarding War Diaries and Intelligence Summaries are contained in F.S. Regs., Part II. and the Staff Manual respectively. Title pages will be prepared in manuscript.

Place	Date	Hour	Summary of Events and Information	Remarks and references to Appendices
LE TOURET	May 10		Attached to 1st Division and grouped with 25th Brigade. Elevating gear of A sub-section gun 21st Battery broke down. Batteries continued fire on German trenches.	
	11		Attached to 7th Division and grouped with 37th Brigade. 6 heavy German shells fell near 21st Battery - no casualties. 22nd Battery fired 6 rounds on P 2 and P 5. Ammunition Column received 1 H.D. from Divisional Ammunition Column.	
	12		Batteries registered new targets on FESTUBERT front.	
	13		22nd Battery fired 8 rounds on "HOUSES" at MOULIN D'EAU. 21st Battery improved gun emplacements.	
	14		21st Battery registered trenches on FESTUBERT front. 22nd Battery fired 12 rounds on P 8 between 9 p.m. 14/5/15 and 3 a.m. 15/5/15. Ammunition Column issued 96 rounds to 22nd Battery and received same from Divisional Ammunition Column. Several enemy shrapnel shells burst in vicinity of Brigade Headquarters.	
	15	8 am	Batteries bombarded German trenches and houses on FESTUBERT front for 3 periods of 2 hours each. Germans, in what appeared to be sailors uniforms, were observed in the trenches on the RICHEBOURG front. Ammunition Column issued 288 rounds to 21st Battery and received same from Divisional Ammunition Column.	
	16	2.45am.	Batteries took part in bombardment of German positions at LA QUINQUE RUE commencing at 2.45 a.m. Observation Station in the RUE DE CAILLOUX, FESTUBERT, was heavily shelled by hostile artillery. Communication with Batteries frequently interrupted by wires being cut. Promptly repaired under fire by Signallers. Gunner Lane, 21st Battery, distinguished himself in repairing the wires under fire. Both Batteries were shelled and Bombardier Milligan, Driver McKnight and Driver Deans of 22nd Battery, were wounded. Driver McKnight died later the same day of his wounds. 2 horses were killed and 2 horses wounded. Bombardment ceased at 4.30 p.m. and registration continued. Ammunition Column issued 96 rounds to 21st Battery and received same from Divisional Ammunition Column.	
		4.30pm.		
	17	5.48am.	Operations continued at 5.48 a.m. 4 rounds were fired on N 15 at 3 p.m. by 22nd Battery. Ammunition Column issued 96 rounds to 21st Battery and received same from Divisional Ammunition Column.	

Army Form C. 2118.

WAR DIARY
or
INTELLIGENCE SUMMARY.

(Erase heading not required.)

Instructions regarding War Diaries and Intelligence Summaries are contained in F. S. Regs., Part II. and the Staff Manual respectively. Title pages will be prepared in manuscript.

Place	Date	Hour	Summary of Events and Information	Remarks and references to Appendices
LE TOURET	May 17		Wagon line in readiness to move. Orders received to unharness at 5.30 p.m.	
	18		22nd Battery continued registration. Intimation received from 5th London Field Ambulance that Driver McKnight of 22nd Battery died of his wounds on the 16th instant and was buried in the Town Cemetery, BETHUNE.	
	19		Gunner Coombes and Gunner Whyte joined Ammunition Column from Base.	
	20	6 pm.	Bombardment started to consolidate new line at FESTUBERT. At 10.30 p.m. Left Section 22nd Battery fired 4 rounds on P 14. Ammunition Column issued 48 rounds to Batteries and received same from Divisional Ammunition Column. Lieut. Smith R.A.M.C. joined the Brigade to relieve Capt. Carmalt Jones R.A.M.C.	
	21		Batteries continued registration. Ammunition Column issued 96 rounds to 21st Battery and received same from Divisional Ammunition Column. Brigade received orders to move to FLEURBAIX at 10.30 p.m. Moved out at 12.30 a.m. 22/5/15 and received orders on the road at 1.30 a.m. to return to positions.	
	22		Batteries continued registration. At 6.20 p.m. 22nd Battery fired 17 rounds on Trench between M 10 and L 12. Ammunition Column issued 96 rounds to 21st Battery and received same from Divisional Ammunition Column. Capt. Carmalt Jones R.A.M.C. left Brigade for Base Hospital Boulogne, and Interpreter de Vissic left Brigade for 3rd Field Company R.E.	
	23		Attached to Canadian Division and grouped with 118th Brigade. Batteries continued registration. Ammunition Column issued 96 rounds to 21st Battery and received same from Divisional Ammunition Column. Interpreter Clericy joined Brigade.	
	24	5 pm. 11.30pm	A slow bombardment of German trenches commenced and at 10.30 p.m. rate of fire increased. Firing ceased. Ammunition Column issued 96 rounds to 22nd Battery and received same from Divisional Ammunition Column.	

Army Form C. 2118.

WAR DIARY
or
INTELLIGENCE SUMMARY.

(Erase heading not required.)

Instructions regarding War Diaries and Intelligence Summaries are contained in F. S. Regs., Part II. and the Staff Manual respectively. Title pages will be prepared in manuscript.

Place	Date	Hour	Summary of Events and Information	Remarks and references to Appendices
LE TOURET	May 25		2/Lt. Spencer and 4 Signallers of 21st Battery assisted in night bombing attack on German trench at FESTUBERT. Ammunition Column issued 96 rounds to 22nd Battery and received same from Divisional Ammunition Column.	
LA MOTTE	26	10 am.	orders received to rejoin 47th (London) Division. Positions reconnoitred near CUINCHY and working parties sent out to prepare emplacements etc. Ammunition Column remained at LES CAUDRONS.	
	27	8 p.m.	21st Battery moved into position on marsh 500 yards South of CUINCHY STATION.	
		9.10pm.	22nd Battery moved into position 700 yards South of CUINCHY STATION. Ammunition Column moved via BETHUNE to BEAUVRY.	
	28		21st Battery moved by sections into new position at LE PLANTIN relieving 47th Battery R.F.A. 22nd Battery registered new targets. Brigade Headquarters moved to GORRE.	
GORRE	29		Batteries continued registration. Several German H.E. shells fell near Brigade Headquarters and among the Batteries. Ammunition Column received 18 rounds from Divisional Ammunition Column to complete 21st Battery Wagon line.	
	30		Received orders to move to VERMELLES. Position at VERMELLES reconnoitred. One section 21st Battery moved to BEAUVRY. Ammunition Column issued 96 rounds to 22nd Battery and received 114 rounds from Divisional Ammunition Column.	
	31		Remaining section of 21st Battery moved to BEAUVRY. Orders received to move into position at VERMELLES. Ammunition Column issued 22 rounds to 21st Battery and received same from Divisional Ammunition Column.	

St. Eley
Lt. Col. R.F.A. T.F.
Officer Commanding,
8th London (How) F.A. Brigade.

121/5931

a-
a16

47th Division

8th London (Hows) Bde RFA.

Vol IV 1 — 30.6.15.

Army Form C. 2118.

WAR DIARY
or
INTELLIGENCE SUMMARY.
(Erase heading not required.)

Instructions regarding War Diaries and Intelligence Summaries are contained in F. S. Regs., Part II. and the Staff Manual respectively. Title pages will be prepared in manuscript.

Place	Date	Hour	Summary of Events and Information	Remarks and references to Appendices
VERMELLES	June 1st		Brigade moved to VERMELLES. Brigade Headquarters established at NOYELLES LES VERMELLES. 21st Battery moved into a position in ruined houses in the centre of the town. Ammunition Column remained at BEAUVRY, and continued walking exercise.	
	2		G.O.C., R.A. inspected gun positions. Batteries registered targets on VERMELLES front. 22nd Battery registered breastworks at G.11 d 7.3.	
	3.		21st Battery registered trenches on VERMELLES front N. of HOHENZOLLERN REDOUBT. The error of 2 of the guns became more marked. 22nd Battery registered trenches G 17 a 8.0 and G 11 a 4.8. The vicinity of the Horse lines having been shelled periodically, the Ammunition Column moved from BEAUVRY at 6 p.m. to LA BOURSE. 7 rounds issued to 21st Battery.	
	4		21st Battery registered parts of the German salient (HOHENZOLLERN REDOUBT) on the VERMELLES front. 22nd Battery registered on Breastworks at G 17 b 5.5 and G 11 b 3.4. There was a violent encounter on our left, apparently CAMBRIN on the night of the 3rd June. Great activity continued on our right in the direction of SOUCHEZ. At 10 a.m. 112 rounds and a new gun wheel were issued to 21st Battery. At 2 p.m. 119 rounds were received from the D.A.C. also a new gun wheel. At 8 p.m. a second new gun wheel was issued to 21st Battery.	
	5		Batteries continued registration. 22nd Battery registered on CROSS ROADS at G 11 d 8.2 and BREASTWORKS G 17 c 8.1. A fierce encounter developed on our right in direction of LOOS About 5 p.m.	
	6	6.30 a.m. 1.15 p.m. 9 p.m.	Ammunition Column issued 86 rounds to 22nd Battery and received a similar number from D.A.C. at 10 a.m. At 1.15 p.m. Brigade received orders to move to rest. Orders regarding 21st Battery afterwards cancelled. At 9 p.m. Headquarters and 22nd Battery left VERMELLES being joined by AMMUNITION Column at LABOURSE at 10 p.m. travelling via VERQUINEUL, VERQUIN, VAUDRICOURT, LABUISSIERE, MARLES, AUCHEL to FERFAY arriving at 4 a.m. Brigade Headquarters established at the MAIRIE.	
FERFAY	7	4 am.	21st Battery moved from VERMELLES and bivouacked at DOUVRIN to await further orders.	

1577 Wt.W10791/1773 500,000 1/15 D.D.&L.   A.D.S.S./Forms/C. 2118.

Army Form C. 2118.

WAR DIARY
or
INTELLIGENCE SUMMARY.
(Erase heading not required.)

Instructions regarding War Diaries and Intelligence Summaries are contained in F. S. Regs., Part II. and the Staff Manual respectively. Title pages will be prepared in manuscript.

Place	Date	Hour	Summary of Events and Information	Remarks and references to Appendices
FERFAY	8 June		21st Battery received orders to move to a position of rest at FERFAY. Guns and carriages were overhauled by the I.O.M. particularly as to the play on the pipe boxes and it was intimated that new pipe boxes or new wheels would be obtained. G.O.C. visited Brigade and congratulated it on its good work in the firing line.	
	9		Lt. Col. E.H.Eley left for England on 7 days leave and Major Eton took over command during his absence. Guns and carriages were inspected by the I.O.M. (Capt. Sparey A.O.C.) Results confirmed examination of previous day.	
	10		Brigade at rest.	
	11		Brigade training. Following reinforcements arrived from BASE:- 531 a/Bomr. Laidlaw 1237 Gunner Fisher 1263 Driver Hayhoe 1046 Joslin 840 Palmer 1041 Stentiford 974 Gunner Wilkenning 1267 Long 886 Llewellen 1136 Waldock 817 Barr 994 Stevens 1000 Sams 1169 Driver Ormiston 928 Hunnable 1337 Waller 1255 Delvin 523 Ward 1133 Childs 1257 Thomas 1302 Fort 544 Stalker Potter	
	12		Brigade at rest. Brigade training carried out.	
	13		Brigade at rest. Brigade training carried out.	
	14		Major General Barter G.O.C. 47th LONDON DIVISION inspected 22nd Battery and Ammunition Column lines.	
	15		Major General Barter G.O.C. 47th LONDON DIVISION inspected 21st Battery lines. 2/Lt. Griffin left for ENGLAND on 8 days leave.	
	16		Brigade at rest. Brigade training carried out.	
	17	1.30am.	Brigade received orders to proceed at ½ hour's notice, to NOUEX LES MINES and there await further orders. Cancelled. Lt. Col. E.H.Eley returned from leave and took over command.	
		4.30am.	instructions.	

Army Form C. 2118.

WAR DIARY
or
INTELLIGENCE SUMMARY.
(Erase heading not required.)

Instructions regarding War Diaries and Intelligence Summaries are contained in F. S. Regs., Part II and the Staff Manual respectively. Title pages will be prepared in manuscript.

Place	Date	Hour	Summary of Events and Information	Remarks and references to Appendices
FERFAY	17 June	5 pm.	Brigade received orders to be ready to move at 1 hour's notice. 1 rider received from D.A.C. and posted to Ammunition Column.	
	18		Brigade in readiness to move. Batteries carry out usual training. Headquarters practice Gun Drill and Signalling.	
	19		Major Eton, Capt. White and Lt. Cooper left for ENGLAND on 7 days leave. Lt. Taylor took over a/Adjutant. Brigade remained in readiness to move.	
	20		Church Service by the Rev. E.H.Bell C.F. in grounds of the CHATEAU. Brigade remained in readiness to move.	
	21	10 am.	Inspection of Brigade in Field Service Marching Order by O.C. Brigade. Orders received to be ready to move at 3 hours' notice.	
	22		Batteries and Ammunition Column carried out Route March of not less than 2 hours' duration. Capt. Largen and Lt. Tomlinson left for ENGLAND on 7 days leave.	
	23		Brigade training carried out.	
	24	4.30 pm.	Orders received to move to new position in Reserve at BOIS DES DAMES. Brigade moved to new position via BURBURE, ALLOUAGNE, LAPUGNOY, LABEUVRIERE, arriving at position at 8 pm. 2/Lt. Griffin returned from leave.	
BOIS DES DAMES	25		2/Lt. Griffin took over a/Adjutant and Lt. Taylor returned to duty with 22nd Battery. Brigade at rest. Lt. Col. E.H.Eley took over duties of G.R.A. temporarily. Veterinary Officer inspected Ammunition Column horses.	
	26		Veterinary Officer inspected Headquarters and Batteries horses.	
	27		Lt. Kindell and Lt. de Witt left for ENGLAND on 7 days leave.	
	28		Major Eton, Capt. White and Lt. Cooper returned from leave. Capt. Cowan left for ENGLAND ON 7 days leave.	

Army Form C. 2118.

WAR DIARY
or
INTELLIGENCE SUMMARY.

(Erase heading not required.)

Instructions regarding War Diaries and Intelligence Summaries are contained in F. S. Regs., Part II and the Staff Manual respectively. Title pages will be prepared in manuscript.

Place	Date	Hour	Summary of Events and Information	Remarks and references to Appendices
Bois des Dames	29 June		Batteries carried out Mounted Drill on HESDIGNEUL Race Course.	
	30		Batteries carried out exercise of not less than 1 hours' duration outside 1st Army area.	

S.W. Eley
Lt. Col. R.F.A. T.F.
Officer Commanding,
8th London (How) F.A. Brigade.

121/6344

47th Division

1/18th London Rule R + R.
Vt V
1 – 3 1 – 4 – 1 5

Army Form C. 2118.

WAR DIARY
or
INTELLIGENCE SUMMARY.

(Erase heading not required.)

Instructions regarding War Diaries and Intelligence Summaries are contained in F. S. Regs., Part II. and the Staff Manual respectively. Title pages will be prepared in manuscript.

Place	Date	Hour	Summary of Events and Information	Remarks and references to Appendices
BOIS DES DAMES.	July 1		Batteries and Headquarters carried out mounted drill on HESDIGNEUL RACECOURSE. Capt. LARGEN and Lieut. TOMLINSON returned from leave. Lt.Col.ELEY resumed command of Brigade on relinquishing duties of acting C.R.A.	
	2		Batteries and Ammunition carried out usual exercises. At 3 p.m. Headquarters practised Gun Drill	
	3		Batteries and Headquarters carried out mounted drill on HESDIGNEUL RACECOURSE. Lieut. SPENCER left for ENGLAND on leave.	
	4	10.40 a.m.	Church Parade held at GOSNAY. Lieut. J.F.SMITH R.A.M.C. left for ENGLAND on leave. Lieut. PLEWS R.A.M.C. assumed duties of Medical Officer.	
GOSNAY	5	8.30 a.m.	Headquarters and 21st Battery moved out of BOIS DES DAMES on account of danger from stray bullets from neighbouring rifle range. Headquarters bivouaced in brickfields and 21st Battery on ground adjoining HESDIGNEUL RACECOURSE. Lieut. DE WITT and Lieut. KINDELL returned from leave.	
	6		Batteries and Headquarters carried out Mounted Drill on HESDIGNEUL RACECOURSE. Major POLLARD, No.1128 Saddler Sergeant MATTHEWS, No.975 Wheeler Sergeant MESSENT, and No.1472 Pte. STILL proceeded to ENGLAND on leave. Lieut. PLEWS R.A.M.C. left to rejoin 5th London F.A. Brigade and Lieut. MCKEEVEL assumed duties of Medical Officer.	
	7		Batteries and Ammunition Column carried out usual training. Capt. COWAN returned from leave.	
	8	9.0 a.m.	Batteries carried out Mounted Drill on HESDIGNEUL RACECOURSE. No.832 Gr. ANDERSONS and No.631 Gr. BRITNELL W. arrived from BASE.	
	9		Batteries carried out usual training. Headquarters practised riding drill.	

Army Form C. 2118.

WAR DIARY
or
INTELLIGENCE SUMMARY.
(Erase heading not required.)

Instructions regarding War Diaries and Intelligence Summaries are contained in F. S. Regs., Part II. and the Staff Manual respectively. Title pages will be prepared in manuscript.

Place	Date	Hour	Summary of Events and Information	Remarks and references to Appendices
GOSNAY	July 10	10a.m.	Brigade inspection by O.C. Headquarters and Batteries on HESDIGNEUL RACECOURSE, Ammunition Column	
		4 p.m.	in Column Park. Orders received for Officers Commanding Batteries to meet C.R.A. to reconnoitre position. 1 Section of 21st Battery sent to 4th Corps A.O.D. travelling workshop for overhauling.	
"		8 p.m.	Headquarters, remaining section of 21st Battery and complete 22nd Battery moved out at 8 p.m. and bivouaced for the night at DROUVIN WOOD. Working parties proceeded to LES BREBIS. Section of 21st Battery with Major ETON and Lieut. DE WITT moved to position in action at FOSSE NO.7.	
DROUVIN WOOD	11	7 p.m.	Headquarters moved to LES BREBIS arriving at 10.30 p.m. At 10 p.m. 22nd Battery moved into position. Wagon Lines established at DROUVIN WOODS. Lieut. SPENCER returned from leave. K.M. Batteries Ammunition Column moved via HESDIGNEUL to DROUVIN WOODS.	
LES BREBIS	12		21st Battery constructed observation station and improved position. Lieut. DE WITT left for a course at the Trench Mortar School at ST VENANT. Received orders at 10 p.m. to be ready to hand	
		12mid night.	over to 48th Division. Orders cancelled at 12 midnight. Right section of Ammunition Column returned to BOIS DES DAMES at 9 p.m. No.952 Gr. SHERWOOD and No./0652/Bomr. TINDALL joined from BASE.	
	13		Right Section of Ammunition Column and Wagon Lines returned to DROUVIN WOODS. Batteries engaged in improving gun emplacements and laying out telephone wires. Lieut. SPENCER attached to section of 21st Battery in action. Lieut. BEVAN left for ENGLAND on leave. 21st Battery registered 4 points in GeRMAN support trenches. 22nd Battery registered one point No.7.Reg. Sergeant Major HOXEY, No.896 Driver FREEMAN left for ENGLAND on leave. Lieut. SMITH R.A.M.C. returned from leave. Lieut. McKEEVIL rejoined 7th London F.A.Bde.	
	14		Major C.A.POLLARD No.957, Wheeler Sergeant MESSENT, and No.1472 Pte. STILL R.A.M.C. returned from leave, No.1128 Saddler Sergeant MATTHEWS having been admitted to MILLBANK BARRACK HOSPITAL, LONDON. 2 guns of 21st Battery returned from A.O.D. travelling Workshops and replaced the two guns in action, which were sent to the ~~Army Corp~~ /Both Batteries continued registration. Ammunition Column issued 16 rounds to 21st Battery and received like amount from the D.A.Column.	

1577 Wt.W10791/1773 500,000 1/15 D.D.&L. A.D.S.S./Forms/C. 2118.

Army Form C. 2118.

WAR DIARY
or
INTELLIGENCE SUMMARY.
(Erase heading not required.)

Instructions regarding War Diaries and Intelligence Summaries are contained in F. S. Regs., Part II. and the Staff Manual respectively. Title pages will be prepared in manuscript.

Place	Date	Hour	Summary of Events and Information	Remarks and references to Appendices
LES BREBIS.	July 15		Batteries continued registration of targets.	
	16		Batteries did not fire; improved gun platforms, etc.	
	17		22nd Battery fired 8 rounds and registered on PUITS No.16.	
	18		21st Battery continued registration. Right Section guns of 22nd Battery sent to A.O.D. workshops and replaced by section of 21st Battery from Workshops.	
	19		Lieut. DE WITT returned from Trench Mortar Course. 22nd Battery fired 4 rounds in retaliation on GERMAN breastwork.	
	20	9 a.m. 1.30 p.m.	Germans shelled Headquarters and town of LES BREBIS with heavy howitzer High Explosive Shell. Several casualties among civilian population. FOSSE No. 6 set on fire by shell fire. Bombardment ceased at 1.30 p.m. 22nd Battery retaliated with 6 rounds on breastwork at M.4.a.2.3. Lieut. SPENCER left 21st Battery to be attached to 22nd Battery. Lieut. TAYLOR, and No.344 Sergeant WOOD left for ENGLAND on leave. 21st Battery registered GERMAN communication trench with aerial observation. Lieut. GRIFFIN transferred to ENGLAND, to report to WAR OFFICE.	
	21	a.m. 10.45	Lieut. BEVAN returned from leave. 22nd Battery position visited by Colonel MCMICKING, O.C. 73rd Brigade, 15th Division. A few GERMAN shells dropped on LES BREBIS at 10.45 a.m. 22nd Battery retaliated with 13 rounds on enemies' breastworks at M.4.a.2.3. and PUITS No.16. 11 men and 24 horses of Headquarters were sent to Wagon Line.	
	22		22nd Battery fired 4 rounds in retaliation on PUITS 16 and registered sap at G.34.a.6.5. Batteries Ammunition Column issued 32 rounds to 21st Battery and received like amount from D.A.Column. 21st Battery fired 8 rounds on Mines and billets at LOOS in retaliation of Germans firing on Electrical Works at MAZINGARBE and on PHILOSOPHE. Enemy shelled GRENAY in afternoon	

Army Form C. 2118.

WAR DIARY
or
INTELLIGENCE SUMMARY.
(Erase heading not required.)

Instructions regarding War Diaries and Intelligence Summaries are contained in F. S. Regs., Part II. and the Staff Manual respectively. Title pages will be prepared in manuscript.

Place	Date	Hour	Summary of Events and Information	Remarks and references to Appendices
LES BREBIS	July 22		(continued) and 22nd Battery retaliated. Enemy fired 30 rounds on FOSSE No.5, of which 18 were blind.	
	23		21st Battery registered G.23.c.29. and G.22.d.10.3. 2 remounts received and placed in charge of Ammunition Column until allocated.	
	24		21st Battery fired 7 rounds and registered G.23.a.4.3. and fired 9 rounds as retaliation. 22nd Battery registered breastwork at G.34.c.45.	
	25	6 p.m.	21st Battery fired 4 rounds on G.23c.29 as ordered by Divisional Artillery. 22nd Battery fired 4 rounds on G.34.c.68, G.34.c.45, M.4.c.64, and M.4.a.13 as ordered by Divisional Artillery C.R.A. 47th Division paid informal early morning visit to 22nd Battery. At 6.30 p.m. 21st Battery	
		5.00"	fired 2 rounds and registered and registered G.23.c.26. At 5.30 p.m. GERMANS shelled PHILOSOPHE with 5.9" howitzer shells which appeared to come from LOOS. At 3.30 p.m.	
		3.30"	31 heavy shell were fired into FOSSE No.5 G.33.c. Batteries Ammunition Column issued 86 rounds to 22nd Battery and like amount from D.A.Column. *Brigade*	
	26	11.20 a.m.	21st. Battery fired 8 rounds on G.28.b.54. as retaliation and at 2.25 p.m. on G.28.b.39. 22nd Battery fired two rounds on PUITS 16 in retaliation. At 6.10 p.m. Heavy Shells passed over 22nd Battery in direction of GRENAY. No.751 a/Bomr. ATKINS W., No.512 Dr. Smith J.M. and No.747 Dr. Sadgrove rejoined from BASE.	
	27		Capt. ADAMS of 2/3rd EAST ANGLICAN (HOW) BRIGADE joined 21st Battery for attachment. At 6.30 p.m. *ADKAMS*	
		6.30 p.m.	21st Battery fired 16 rounds on trench G.22.d and G.28.b in co-operation with Infantry. No.24,0005.M.Langton No.80 B.Q.M.S.Davy and No.866 Gr.Furze left for ENGLAND on leave.	
		11 p.m.	Right section 22nd Battery releived by section of B Battery 73rd Brigade and moved to woods adjoining chateau MONT EVENIC. Batteries Ammunition Column issued 42 rounds to 21st Battery and 10 to 22nd Battery and drew 52 rounds from D.A.Column. *Brigade*	

Army Form C. 2118.

WAR DIARY
or
INTELLIGENCE SUMMARY.
(Erase heading not required.)

Instructions regarding War Diaries and Intelligence Summaries are contained in F. S. Regs., Part II. and the Staff Manual respectively. Title pages will be prepared in manuscript.

Place	Date	Hour	Summary of Events and Information	Remarks and references to Appendices
LES BREBIS	July 28	8 a.m.	21st Battery fired 5 rounds on G.28.b.36 in retaliation. Right section of 22nd Battery arrived at woods adjoining chateau MONT EVENIC.	
	29		21st Battery fired on LOOS in retaliation. At 8 p.m. Headquarters moved to woods adjoining chateau MONT EVENIC. Left section of 22nd Battery relieved by section of B Battery 73rd Brigade and moved from LES BREBIS at 10 p.m. arriving at MONT EVENIC at 8.15a.m. 30/7/15.	
MONT EVENIC	30		21st Battery position at FOSSE No.7 was shelled by 77 m.m. gun and 10.5 c.m. How. about 30 rounds being fired. Buildings were hit but no casualties to personnel or material.	
	31		21st Battery fired on LOOS in retaliation.	

LT. COLONEL R.F.A.(T.F.)
COMMANDING 8TH LONDON (HOWR.) ...

121/6754

47th Division

1/15th London Rde: R.F.H.
Got VI
August. 15.

Army Form C. 2118.

WAR DIARY
or
INTELLIGENCE-SUMMARY.
(Erase heading not required.)

Instructions regarding War Diaries and Intelligence Summaries are contained in F. S. Regs., Part II. and the Staff Manual respectively. Title pages will be prepared in manuscript.

Place	Date	Hour	Summary of Events and Information	Remarks and references to Appendices
MONT EVENIC Ref. Map. D.19.a 36 B, N.E. 1/20,000.	August 1		Brigade in Reserve. One Section of D 73 Battery, (4.5" Howitzers) arrived at Fosse No.7 to relieve section of 21st Battery. Brigade Ammunition Column issued 36 rounds to 21st Battery and drew similar amount from Divisional Ammunition Column.	
	2		21st Battery moved to reserve at MONT EVENIC. Capt. ABNAMS, 2/3rd East Anglian Brigade R.F.A. reattached to 73rd Brigade. Brigade training carried out. Driver C.M.Smith, Headquarters, returned from Field Ambulance. Gunner F.H.Jones, 21st Battery returned to duty from Hospital. Sergt. J.Avery and Dr. J.B.Scott, 22nd Battery admitted to Field Ambulance.	
	3	4 pm.	Major E.ETON and Sergt. WARNER, 21st Battery granted 7 days leave of absence. At 4 pm. Brigade Ammunition Column left DROUVIN WOOD for MONT EVENIC, LAPUGNOY, arriving at 7 pm. Capt. E.C.WHITE and Gr.HUNTINGFORD, Ammunition Column, admitted to Field Ambulance.	
	4		Brigade Training carried out. Bathing Parades at AUCHEL at 9.30 am. and 1.30 pm. Driver WEBB Ammunition Column discharged from Field Ambulance.	
	5		Brigade training as detailed in Sketch of Training by G0.C. 47th/Division commenced. 2 N.C.O.s and 22men exchanged with each Battery from Brigade Ammunition Column for training. Bathing Parades at 1.30 pm.	
	6			
	7		Brigade training carried out.	
	8	11am.	O.C. Brigade inspected lines of Units at 11 am. Brigade Ammunition Column issued 15 rounds to 21st Battery and 8 rounds to 22nd Battery and drew 23 rounds from Divisional Ammunition Column. Church Parade at MARLES LES MINES. Gunner Stewart, 21st Battery, admitted to Field Ambulance. Capt. E.C.White, Ammunition Column returned from Field Ambulance.	
	9		Working Party of 75 men (including proportion of N.C.O.s) and 2 Officers left Brigade to prepare gun positions in neighbourhood of MAZINGARBE.	

Army Form C. 2118.

WAR DIARY
or
INTELLIGENCE SUMMARY.
(Erase heading not required.)

Instructions regarding War Diaries and Intelligence Summaries are contained in F. S. Regs., Part II. and the Staff Manual respectively. Title pages will be prepared in manuscript.

Summary of Events and Information 2.

Place	Date	Hour	Summary of Events and Information	Remarks and references to Appendices
MONT EVENIC	August 9		Batteries carried out Mounted Drill on HESDIGNEUL Racecourse. Headquarters carried out Riding Drill in Field at MONT EVENIG.	
	10		Capt. E.C.WHITE transferred from Brigade Ammunition Column to Divisional Ammunition Column. B.S.M. J.CRAIG, Sergt. MOORE and Dr. DAVIS, granted 7 days leave of absence.	
	11		Brigade training carried out. Dr. SCOTT, 22nd Battery, returned from Field Ambulance.	
	12		Major E.ETON and Sergt. WARNER, returned from leave. Brigade training carried out. Brigade training carried out. Helio Station arranged with 47th Divisional Artillery. Communication established at 2 pm.	
	13	9 a.m.	Batteries carried out Mounted Drill on HESDIGNEUL Race course.	
	14		Brigade training carried out.	
	15	11am.	Church Parade held at MARLES LES MINES.	
	16		Lt. K.WEBSTER, joined Brigade from 2/8th London (How) Bde. R.F.A. 1st Party of 25 men proceeded to LES BREBIS to relieve Working Party. Dr. C.M.SMITH, and Gr. W.E.FRASER, Headquarters admitted to Field Ambulanc e. Far. Sgt. ANNETT, Ammunition Colum admitted to Field Ambulance.	
	17		Batteries carried out Mounted Drill on HESDIGNEUL Racecourse. B.Q.M.S.CHAMBERLAIN, StaffSergt. LAURENCE, STaff Sergt. STYLES, Gr. WHITEHEAD and Gr. REID granted 7days leave. 2nd relief party of 25 men proceeded to LES BREBIS.	

1577 Wt.W10791/1773 500,000 1/15 D.D.&L.   A.D.S.S./Forms/C. 2118.

Army Form C. 2118.

WAR DIARY
or
INTELLIGENCE SUMMARY.
(Erase heading not required.)

Instructions regarding War Diaries and Intelligence Summaries are contained in F.S. Regs., Part II. and the Staff Manual respectively. Title pages will be prepared in manuscript.

Summary of Events and Information 3.

Place	Date	Hour	Summary of Events and Information	Remarks and references to Appendices
MONT EVENIC	August 18		B.S.M. J.CRAIG, Sergt. MOORE, Dr. DAVIS, returned from leave. 3 Gun detachments with Major POLLARD Lt. DE WITT and Lt. SPENCER attached to 15th Div. ARTY. for training with 4.5" Howitzers.	
	19		3rd Relief Party of 25 men proceeded to LES BREBIS. Brigade training carried out.	
	20		Brigade training carried out.	
	21		2/Lt. A.L.LAWTHER joined Brigade from 3rd Line Depot. At 11am. O.C. Brigade inspected Units in their lines. B.S.M. J. CRAIG promoted R.S.M. Wh. Sergt. COOMBES, Ammunition Column admitted to Field Ambulance.	
	22	11am.	Church Parade at MARLES LES MINES. Capt. COWAN, 21st Battery to Brigade Ammunition Column vice Capt. WHITE, to Divisional Ammunition Column. Lt. K.WEBSTER posted to 21st Battery. 2/Lt. A.L.LAWTHER posted to Brigade Headquarters as Orderly Officer.	
	23		Inspection of transport. Brigade training carried out.	
	24		Lt. E.R.Cooper, granted 7 days leave of absence. Brigade training carried out. Gr. F.F.WILKINSON 21st Battery to Field Ambulance.	
	25		Divisional Sports at LAPUGNOY. Brigade granted a holiday. Sergt. HENLEY and Corpl. BEAL granted leave. B.Q.M.S. CHAMBERLAIN, Staff Sergeant STYLES, Staff Sergeant LAWRENCE, Gr.	

1577 Wt.W10791/1773 500,000 1/15 D.D. & L.   A.D.S.S./Forms/C. 2118.

Army Form C. 2118.

WAR DIARY
or
INTELLIGENCE SUMMARY.
(Erase heading not required.)

Instructions regarding War Diaries and Intelligence Summaries are contained in F. S. Regs., Part II. and the Staff Manual respectively. Title pages will be prepared in manuscript.

Place	Date	Hour	Summary of Events and Information	Remarks and references to Appendices
MONT EVENIC	25		Gr. WHITEHEAD, Gr. REID returned from leave. 1 Remount received. Corpl.S.S. J.BARRETT joined from BASE.	
	26		Brigade O.C./reconoitred for new positions. Gun detachments with 15th Divisional Artillery changed.	
	27		O.C. Brigade inspected all equipment of wagons and carts for technical tools. Establishment complete. Brigade training carried out.	
	28		Driver JEFFREY granted seven days leave of absence. Brigade training carried out. Sergeant WOOD, Ammunition Column admitted to Field Ambulance.	
	29		Church Parade at MARLES LES MINES, after which Brigade marched past C.O.C.R.A. Lieut. R.DE WITT 21st Battery promoted Captain and posted to 21st Battery. O.C. Brigade and Major E.ETON attended conference at 11 a.m. at MAZINGARBE and proceeded to carry out reconnaisance for additional gun positions.	
	30		Brigade training carried out.	
	31		Brigade training carried out. At 6.10 p.m. orders received to vacate position at MONT EVENIC on the morrow.	

S.R.Cooper E. Marr
for Lt. Col. R.F.A. T.F.
Commanding, 8th Lon (How) F. A. Brigade.

1577 Wt.W10791/1773 500,000 1/15 D.D.&L. A.D.S.S./Forms/C. 2118.

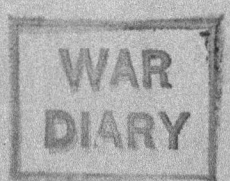

Headquarters,

235th BRIGADE, R.F.A.
(1/8 London)

(47th Division)

S E P T E M B E R

1 9 1 5

Army Form C. 2118.

WAR DIARY
or
INTELLIGENCE SUMMARY

(Erase heading not required.)

Instructions regarding War Diaries and Intelligence Summaries are contained in F.S. Regs., Part II. and the Staff Manual respectively. Title pages will be prepared in manuscript.

Place	Date	Hour	Summary of Events and Information	Remarks and references to Appendices
DROUVIN WOODS.	Sept. 1st	3.30 p.m.	The Headquarters and Batteries moved from MONT EVENIC at 3.30 p.m. and arrived at DROUVIN at 5.45 p.m. and there went into bivouacs. The Brigade Ammunition Column moved from LAPUGNOY at 2.30 p.m. and bivouaced at HAILLICOURT. Captain DE WITT admitted to Hospital. Lieutenant E.R.COOPER returned from 7 days leave of absence. Lieutenant R.G.TOMLINSON returned from attachment to 73rd Brigade R.F.A. Lieutenant H.SPENCER went on Divisional Communications.	
	2nd	7.15 p.m.	Major E.ETON reconnoitred for observing stations overlooking area LOOS and HULLUCH. 22nd Battery moved from DROUVIN at 7.15 p.m. and arrived at the position originally occupied at LES BREBIS - L.35.d.5.5. - at 10 p.m. the wagon lines remaining at DROUVIN.	
	3rd		Captain A.J.COWAN and Lieutenant H.SPENCER of Brigade Ammunition Column attached for duty to 21st Battery, Major E.ETON attended conference at MAZINGARBE. 22nd Battery worked on gun positions and established telephone communication with Observing Station at South MAROC - M.8.b.8.9.	
	4th		22nd Battery re-registered all guns on original line, trench at foot of DOUBLE CRASSIER - M.4.a.1.3. Registered No.1 gun on PUITS 16 - M.10.a.5.0. Brigade Ammunition Column issued 192 complete rounds to 22nd Battery. No.2604 Corporal Shoeing Smith J.BARRETT reverted to Gunner at his own request and was transferred to 21st Battery.	
LES BREBIS	5th		22nd Battery improved gun positions etc. No.520 Driver T.VILES, Headquarters, returned from Field Ambulance. No.1243 Driver B.JEFFREY, Headquarters, returned from 7 days leave of absence.	
	6th		Lt.Colonel E.H.ELEY appointed Group Commander for Howitzers, Southern Group - 22nd (How) Battery R.F.A. and 23rd Siege Battery R.G.A. forming the Group. Change from 50 pr. shell to 40 pr. shell commenced. Brigade Ammunition Column returned 368 rounds 50 lb. Ammunition to Divisional Ammunition Column and received 368 rounds 40 lb Ammunition in exchange. 50 rounds of 40 lb Ammunition issued to 22nd Battery Firing Line and	

1577 Wt.W10791/1773 500,000 1/15 D.D.&L. A.D.S.S./Forms/C. 2118.

Army Form C. 2

Instructions regarding War Diaries and Intelligence Summaries are contained in F. S. Regs., Part II. and the Staff Manual respectively. Title pages will be prepared in manuscript.

WAR DIARY or INTELLIGENCE SUMMARY

(Erase heading not required.)

Place	Date	Hour	Summary of Events and Information	Remarks and references to Appendices
LES BREBIS	Sept. 6th		50 rounds of 50lb. ammunition received in exchange. 21st Battery moved into position 100 yards South of the GRENAY - MAROC Road - M.2.c.6.0. Sheet 36.0. The Battery was grouped under Lt. Col. MACNAGHTEN R.F.A. with Lt. Col. SHARP as Howitzer Sub-Group Commander for offensive operations impending. Interpreter C.CLERICY granted 7 days leave of absence.	
	7th		Capt. F. DE WITT discharged from Hospital and rejoined 21st Battery. Capt. A.J.COWAN rejoined Brigade Ammunition Column. A working party was detailed to prepare new forward position for 22nd Battery in South MAROC - M.2.d.8.8. Right section of Battery registered on Eastern End of DOUBLE CRASSIER - M.5.c.5.0. Left Section registered on communication trench at M.4.d.1.4. 318 rounds of 50lb. ammunition were returned to Divisional Ammunition Column. 1 G.S. Wagon was returned by 22nd Battery.	
	8th		21st Battery took over duties in line of defence from 40th Battery R.F.A. Left Section of 22nd Battery registered on communication trench at M.4.d.9.1. Right Section registered on communication trench at M.10.b.1.5. Lt. Col. E.H.ELEY reconnoitred advance positions for 40th Battery and 22nd Battery. The following N.C.O.s and men proceeded to ENGLAND on 7 days leave of absence. B.S.M. SALE, Wh.Sgt. MITCHELL, Corpl. CARTER, Corpl. CROUCH, Corpl.MILES, a/Br. BYRON, Dr. DUNN Trmptr. PRICE. 96 rounds of 40lb. ammunition taken to 21st Battery - 96 rounds of 50lb. ammunition returned to Ammunition Column. 318 rounds of 50lb. ammunition returned to Divisional Ammunition Column, 400 rounds of 40 lb ammunition received from Divisional Ammunition Column. 144 rounds of 40 lb 96 rounds 50 lb ammunition returned to Divisional Ammunition Column. 96 rounds returns of 40 lb ammunition issued to 21st Battery Wagon Line. 96 rounds of 50 lb ammunition returned to Divisional Ammunition Column. 80 rounds of 40 lb ammunition issued to 22nd Battery Wagon Line. 80 rounds of 50 lb ammunition returned to Divisional Ammunition Column.	
	9th		Lieutenant E.R.COOPER reconnoitred for visual signalling stations between 22nd Observation Station and Headquarters.	

Army Form C. 2118

Instructions regarding War Diaries and Intelligence Summaries are contained in F.S. Regs., Part II. and the Staff Manual respectively. Title pages will be prepared in manuscript.

WAR DIARY or INTELLIGENCE SUMMARY.

(Erase heading not required.)

Place	Date	Hour	Summary of Events and Information	Remarks and references to Appendices
LES BREBIS	Sept. 9th		21st Battery commenced retaliating on all German shelling of our line west of LOOS and registered various points in German front line trenches, support and communication trenches and second line trenches between LOOS and the DOUBLE CRASSIER of FOSSE No.11 de LENS. This was continued up to the 20/9/15. Right section of 22nd Battery registered on communication trenches at M.10.a.8.2. and M.10.a.9.3.	
	10th		22nd Battery improved gun platforms etc.	
	11th		The right section of 22nd Battery fired on targets at M.11.a.3.1. and M.10.d.5.6. with aeroplane observation. No.3 gun fired on DOUBLE CRASSIER. No.1 gun fired at 8.30 p.m. on enemy's transport reported by Infantry at M.10.d. 68 rounds 40 lb ammunition issued to 22nd Battery.	
	12th		No.3 gun of 22nd Battery registered on front line trench at M.4.c.6.9. and M.4.a.5.0. 259 rounds of 50 lb ammunition and 234 rounds of 40 lb ammunition were received by Brigade Ammunition Column from Divisional Ammunition Column. 45 rounds of 40 lb ammunition issued to 21st Battery Wagon Line. 446 rounds of 40 lb ammunition issued to 22nd Battery Wagon Line.	
	13th		Advanced wagon line established at NOEUX LES MINES. 1st line wagons at HAILLICOURT. Headquarters wagon line also moved to HAILLICOURT.	
	14th		No.599 Sergeant HORNER and No.147 Gunner BERTRAM, 22nd Battery granted 6 days leave of absence. 160 rounds of 50 lb ammunition issued to 22nd Battery wagon line. 48 rounds of 40 lb ammunition returned from 22nd Battery wagon line to Brigade Ammunition Column. 440 rounds 40 lb ammunition returned to Divisional Ammunition xxxxxx Park. Interpreter C. CLERICY returned from leave.	
	15th		22nd Battery moved to new forward position in SOUTH MAROC - M.2.d.8.8. 22nd Battery gun No.52 sent xxxxxxxxxx for repair to springCases to No.1 Workshop, Army Ordnance Depot.	

Army Form C. 2?

INTELLIGENCE SUMMARY

or

[Erase heading not required.]

Instructions regarding War Diaries and Intelligence Summaries are contained in F.S. Regs., Part II. and the Staff Manual respectively. Title pages will be prepared in manuscript.

Place	Date	Hour	Summary of Events and Information	Remarks and references to Appendices
LES BREBIS	Sept. 15th		159 rounds of 50 lb ammunition received from Divisional Ammunition Column. 85 rounds of 40 lb ammunition returned to Divisional Ammunition Column. 27 rounds of 40 lb ammunition issued to 21st Battery Wagon Line. 74 rounds of 40 lb ammunition returned to Brigade Ammunition Column from 22nd Battery wagon line. 49 rounds of 50 lb ammunition issued to 22nd Battery wagon line. No.471 Gunner R.J.W.HOMAN, Brigade Ammunition Column and No.678 Gunner H.ELLIS, 22nd Battery granted 5 days leave of absence.	
	16th		No.4 gun 22nd Battery fired on communication trench. 209 rounds of 50 lb ammunition and 12 rounds of 40 lb ammunition issued to 21st Battery wagon line. B.S.M. SALE N.X.Wheeler-Sergeant MITCHELL, Corporal MILES, Corporal CARTER, Corporal CROUCH, a/Bombardier BYRON, Trumpeter PRICE, and Driver DUNN returned from 7 days leave. No.769 Shoeing-Smith CLEVELAND granted 4 days leave of absence.	
	17th		Officer Commanding Brigade attended a conference at Divisional Artillery with C.R.A. IVth Corps. 249 rounds of 40 lb ammunition received from Divisional Ammunition Column and 250 rounds of 40lb ammunition issued to 22nd Battery wagon line. 100 "T" tubes issued to 21st Battery wagon line.	
	18th		22nd Battery improved positions etc.	
	19th		173 rounds of 40 lb ammunition received from Divisional Ammunition. 169 rounds of 40 lb ammunition issued to 21st Battery Wagon line.	
	20th		Conference at Brigade Headquarters between Officer Commanding Brigade, Major POLLARD, 22nd Battery, and Major LOCKHART of 23rd Siege Battery. Afterwards Officer Commanding Brigade attended conference at Headquarters SOUTHERN GROUP. At 11 a.m. the group carried out a test and each battery fired 1 round. About 4 p.m. No.749 Gunner E.JACKSON, 21st Battery, whilst returning to the Battery position, went, in company with Colonel BUTCHER R.F.A., to the assistance of a civilian who had been wounded by an enemy shell, at the cross roads close to GRENAY Church. A second enemy shell falling close to the first, killed all three.	

Place	Date	Hour	Summary of events and information	Remarks & refs: to Appendices
LES BREBIS	Sept 20th		Signalling class commenced in Brigade Ammunition Column under Corporal MILES of Brigade Headquarters. 57 rounds 40 lb ammunition issued to 21st Battery.	
	21st	8 a.m.	Bombardment commenced. 21st Battery bombarded section of German defences EAST and SOUTH of LOOS and to NORTH of DOUBLE CRASSIER of FOSSE No.11 de LENS. The 22nd Battery fired upon the following points in the enemy's trenches and billets in CITE ST. PIERRE. - M.11.a.6.5., M.10.d.5.6., M.4.d.3.8.,-M.5.c.5.0., M.4.c.4.9. through M.4.d.1.3. to EAST END of DOUBLE CRASSIER, SOUTH portion of DOUBLE CRASSIER to M.4.c.4.9., M.10.a.6.7.,- M.10.b.2.5., M.4.d.1.4.- M.10.a.7.6.,M.10.b.0.3. through M.4.d.9.3. - M.5.c.5.0. 600 rounds 40 lb ammunition received from Divisional Ammunition Column and 600 rounds 40 lb ammunition issued to 21st Battery 196 rounds 40 lb ammunition issued to 22nd Battery	
	22nd		Bombardment continued. Both batteries fired on same targets as yesterday according to programme The objectives of the 21st Battery were communication trench in G.34.b.1.2. to G.34.b.5.5. houses in G.34.b.c and d, G.35.d. and G.36.c. Trenches G.35.c.5.1. to G.35.a.6.3 (including LOOS cemetery) G.35.d.9.1.; the railway cutting M.6.b. to M.6.d. the chalk Pit in M.6.a. and the copse M.5.b. to M.6.a., Trenches G.35.c.7.5. to G.35.d.6.1.; G.35.c.9.8. to G.35.d.9.1. The 22nd Battery preceded their bombardment by one round of Battery fire on communication trenches M.5.a.2.6.-G.35.c.6.3. and two rounds of battery fire on front line trench M.4.a.2.3 - In addition the battery fired on front line trench about M.10.a.5.6. at 2 p.m. (M.4.a.8.7. 484 rounds of 40 lb ammunition were received from Divisional Ammunition Column. 288 rounds of 40 lb ammunition were issued to 22nd Battery. 30 "T" tubes issued to 21st Battery. 37 rounds of 40 lb ammunition received from Divisional Ammunition Column and issued to 22nd Battery.	
	23rd		Bombardment continued. Batteries fired on same targets as yesterday from 8 a.m. to 5 p.m. according to programme.	

WAR DIARY

Place	Date	Hour	Summary of events and information	Remarks & refs: to Appendices
LES BREBIS	Sept 23rd		In addition to usual targets, 22nd Battery fired on head of new communication trench at M.11.a.2.8. entrance to DOUBLE CRASSIER at M.5.c.0.4. and entrance to Railway embankment at M.10.b.1.3. 126 rounds of 40 lb ammunition received from Divisional Ammunition Column.	
	24th		Bombardment continued on same target as yesterday according to programme from 8 a.m. to 5.15 p.m. in addition to usual task, 22nd battery fired on front line and communication trenches along the South of the DOUBLE CRASSIER about 2 p.m. 126 rounds of 40 lb ammunition were issued to 21st Battery. During the period of bombardment a large number of misfires occurred owing to faulty friction tubes. Several drag shoe chains or shoes were broken and one nipple-buffer tube connecting broke.	
	25th		The day of assault. Zero time was 4.50 a.m. 21st Battery fired for 40 minutes upon the trenches in G.34.b.1.2. to G.34.b.5.5. and G.35.c.5.1. to G.35.a.6.3. (called the cemetery trench) in preparation for the Infantry assault. The 22nd Battery opened fire at 5.50 a.m. on the enemy's front line trenches. Continued fire throughout the day until about 6 p.m. on front line and communication trenches in zone south of DOUBLE CRASSIER. At the moment of the Infantry assault, 6.30 a.m., the fire of 21st Battery was lifted on to the enclosure (corons) in G.34, at the new school in LOOS (G.35.d.7.8.) for 25 minutes and thence the fire lifted again on to trenches connecting the copse in M.5.b. to the mine railway in M.6.c. until 7.20 a.m. At 7.20 a.m. until 11.15 a.m. fire was again lifted on to the trenches in the CORONS of FOSSE No.11 (M.6.c.) to form a barrage. The objectives of the 47th (London) Division in the attack South of LOOS having been attained, some units of the MACNAGHTEN Group were moved up in support of the Infantry who had advanced North of LOOS and the 21st Battery was at noon transferred to the MASSY Group of Artillery who were dealing with the Sector S. of the DOUBLE CRASSIER of FOSSE 11, which formed the right defensive flank and pivot of the general attack. 500 rounds of 40 lb ammunition were received from Divisional Ammunition Column. 252 rounds of 40 lb ammunition issued to 21st Battery and 248 rounds of 40 lb ammunition issued to 22nd Battery.	
	26th		21st Battery remained in MASSY Group and fired when called upon in forming barrages along the mine railway running E. from DOUBLE CRASSIER during isolated actions. The 21st Battery fired occasionally upon German front line and communication trenches between DOUBLE CRASSIER and	

"W A R D I A R Y.
****

Place	Date	Hour	Summary of events and information.	Remarks & refs: to Appendices
LES BREBIS	Sept 26th		PUITS No.16 de LENS. The 22nd Battery commenced firing at 9 a.m. a barrage on North of railway on line N.l.a.-N.2.a. During the afternoon the Battery fired on the enemy's works and emplacements on HILL 70 on west side of LENS - LA BASSEE Road. 204 rounds of 40 lb ammunition received from Divisional Ammunition Column. 122 rounds of 40 lb ammunition issued to 21st Battery and 82 rounds of 40 lb ammunition issued to 22nd Battery. 70 rounds of 50 lb ammunition received from Divisional Ammunition Column and issued to 21st Battery.	
	27th		21st Battery continued to fire when called upon as yesterday. 22nd Battery commenced firing at 9.55 a.m. and shelled the copse in M.6.a. and fired the same barrage as previous day until 7.35 p.m. 648 rounds 40 lb ammunition were received from Divisional Ammunition Column and issued to 22nd Battery. 230 rounds of 50 lb received from Divisional Ammunition Column and issued to 22nd Battery. 148 rounds of 40 lb ammunition received from Divisional Ammunition Column. 89 rounds rounds of 40 lb ammunition issued to 21st Battery and 59 rounds of 40 lb ammunition to 22nd Battery.	
	28th		21st Battery continued barraging along the same line as yesterday. The 22nd Battery fired a few rounds at enemy's cavalry on LENS - LA BASSEE Road. 675 rounds of 50 lb ammunition received from Divisional Ammunition Column and issued 384 rounds to 21st Battery and 291 rounds to 22nd Battery. No.1128 Sad.Sergeant MATTHEWs rejoined Brigade from 3rd Line Depot, with 15 reinforcements. No.1082 Trumpeter W.J.YOUNG, Headquarters, mustered as a Gunner and transferred to Brigade Ammunition Column.	
	29th		21st Battery continued its barrage. 1 H.D. horse No.17079, Ammunition Column, died. No.767 Dr.L.LANGLEY, Headquarters, admitted to Field Ambulance with injured foot.	
	30th		21st Battery moved forward to a position in North MAROC (G.35.d.6.7.) in closer support of Infantry who were then established in a line East of LOOS. 22nd Battery fired a few rounds on barrage north of railway M.6.d. and on cross roads in CITE ST EDOUARD M.6.a.7.2.	

H. Wey
LT. COLONEL R.F.A.(T.F.)
COMMANDING 8th LONDON (HOW) F.A. BRIGADE

Army Form C. 2118.

WAR DIARY
****

Place	Date	Hour	Summary of events and information	Remarks & refs: to Appendices
LES BREBIS	Sept		**REMARKS BY BRIGADE MEDICAL OFFICER.**	

During the month of September the health of the troops under my medical supervision has remained excellent. There were no cases of epidemic disease. There were three cases of scabies sent to Field Ambulance on September 4th, but the measures taken were sufficient to prevent any further spread of this affection. Since September 5th the Ammunition Column and Wagon Lines, being separated from the Batteries, have not been under my charge.

On September 25th at various times during the morning I treated about ten soldiers suffering from gas-poisoning, apparently due to our own gas. The main symptoms were nausea, abdominal pain thirst, and a rapid thready pulse. In one only was there marked respiratory trouble. There was no loss of consciousness in any case and no cyanosis. In a large number of wounded enemy prisoners one only complained of gas-poisoning, and as he was in addition suffering from a severe chest wound it was impossible to appraise the effects of the gas. Inhalations of Ammonia had no appreciable effect on the condition.

WAR DIARY

Summary of events and information

Place	Date	Hour	Summary of events and information	Remarks & refs: to Appendices
LES BREBIS	Sept		**REMARKS BY BRIGADE MEDICAL OFFICER.** During the month of September the health of the troops under my medical supervision has remained excellent. There were no cases of epidemic disease. There were three cases of scabies sent to Field Ambulance on September 4th, but the measures taken were sufficient to prevent any further spread of this affection. Since September 5th the Ammunition Column and Wagon Lines, being separated from the Batteries, have not been under my charge. On September 25th at various times during the morning I treated about ten soldiers suffering from gas-poisoning, apparently due to our own gas. The main symptoms were nausea, abdominal pain thirst, and a rapid thready pulse. In one only was there marked respiratory trouble. There was no loss of consciousness in any case and no cyanosis. In a large number of wounded enemy prisoners one only complained of gas-poisoning, and as he was in addition suffering from a severe chest wound it was impossible to appraise the effects of the gas. Inhalations of Ammonia had no appreciable effect on the condition.	

47TH DIVISION

238/9 E

21 ST LONDON BTY R.F.A.
SEP 1915.

47TH DIVISION

238th Brigade, R.F.A.
(1/8 London)

47th Division.

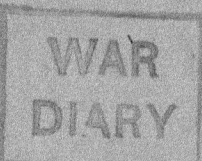

21st LONDON BATTERY, R.F.A.

SEPTEMBER

1915

Instructions regarding War Diaries and Intelligence Summaries are contained in F.S. Regs., Part II. and the Staff Manual respectively. Title pages will be prepared in manuscript.

Army Form C.2118.

INTELLIGENCE SUMMARY.
(Erase heading not required.)

21st London Battery R.F.A.

Place	Date	Hour	Summary of Events and Information	Remarks and references to Appendices
	1/9/1915		Battery moved position in readiness at Drouvin. Captain de Witt to hospital, sick.	
	2/9/1915		Reconnoitred Railway Station overlooking area LOOS & HULLOCH.	
	3/9/1915		Captain Cowan 8th Lda A.C. & Lieut Spencer 8th Lda A.C. attached for duty to 21 Battery.	
	4/9/1915		All 50 lb. lyddite shell returned through field echelon & new 50 lb. ammunition (lyddite) with new cordite cartridges issued. Effect increase range of 5" howitzer to 6,100 yards. Battery burrowed rifle action in position 100 yards south of the Gorres-Mazoc road (map reference M.2.c.6.0 Sheet 36.C.). The Battery grouped under McNaughten's with Lieut Colonel Sharp as Howitzer Sub group commander for Hazrain Franklin undertaking. Captain de Witt discharged from hospital returned battery. Captain Cowan ordered to rejoin HAC.	
	5/9/15 to 8/9/15		Battery took over duties in his defence from 460th Battery R.F.A.	
	20/9/15		Battery detailed on all German staffing to west of LOOS and registered various points in German front line trenches, support & communication trenches and second line trenches between LOOS and the Double Crassier of FOSSE No 11 de Lens.	
	21/9/15 to 24/9/15		Battery took part in bombardment of section of German defences East and South	

1577 Wt.W10791/1773 500,000 1/15 D.D. & L. A.D.S.S./Forms/C. 2118.

INTELLIGENCE SUMMARY.
(Erase heading not required.)

Place	Date	Hour	Summary of Events and Information	Remarks and references to Appendices
			6 LOOS 1 to North of double crassier of FOSSE No. 11. de LENS. 11 Th. Artillery Bomb:	
			Preliminary bombardment of 4 days 1 night, fired 1440 rounds upon the following	
			Chief objectives. Communication trench in S.34 B.1.2 to S.34 B.5.5; trenches in S.34	
			B.C. & D, & 35 D & 36 C. Trenches S.35 C.5.1 to 9.35 a.6.3 (including LOOS Cemetery),	
			9.35.C.7.5 to 9.35.D.6.1. 9.35.D.9.8 to 9.35.D.9.1. The railway cutting in 6.A.S. & n.6.D.	
			the Chalk Pit in h.6.a. and the Copse h.5.B. trenches A.11 from the period some	
			500 minors occurred on & faulty friction tubes. 14 Bay Shown Chain or shoes	
			been broken, + one hipple-hipple-tube connecting tube.11	
25/9/15	5.50am		The Battery fired for 40 minutes upon the trenches in S.34 B.1.2 to S.34 B.5.5	
			and 9.35 C.5.1 to 9.35 C.6.3 (called the Cemetery trench) in preparation for the	
			Infantry assault. At the moment 1st Inf. to assault 6.30am the fire was	
			lifted on to the enclosure (corons) in S.34 at the new school in LOOS (9.35a.7.8)	
			for 25 minutes, + thence the fire lifted again on to trenches connecting the	
			copse in h.5.B. to the mine workings in h.6.c. until 7.20 am. At 7.20 am	
			until 11.15 am fire was again lifted on to the trenches in the corons	
			of FOSSE No 11. (h.6.C.) to form a barrage. From evidence obtained from	

INTELLIGENCE SUMMARY.

(Erase heading not required.)

Place	Date	Hour	Summary of Events and Information	Remarks and references to Appendices
	26.9.15 to 28.9.15		our infantry officers who went into the trenches in S.34.B and on towards French which the 21st London Batty had dealt with, pretending the fire had been most effective — both trenches being practically filled in to considerable lengths. The objective of the 47th (London) Division in the attack south of LOOS having been attained, some units of the Naughton group were moved up in support of the Infantry who had advanced north of LOOS. 7th & London Batty was at now transferred to the Massy Group of artillery who were shortly dealing with the sector S.of the Double Crassis of Loos-Hoen from which formed the right defensive flank & pivot of the general attack. Battery remained in (Noeux) defensive group upon i form barrages along the main Railway running E. from Double Crassis during isolated infantry actions. Battery fired occasionally upon German front line & communication trenches between Double Crassis and Puit No 16. de LENS.	
	30/9/15		Battery moved forward to a position in NORTH MAROC (S.35.d.6.7) in close support of Infantry who were now established in a line — East of LOOS	

Cortay or Xxxxxx Butler RFA191 T.
Commy or Xxxxxx Butler RFA 191 T.

238th Bde. R.F.A.
(1/8 London)
47th Div.

WAR DIARY

22nd LONDON BATTERY, R.F.A.

SEPTEMBER

1915

Army Form C. 2118.

Page 1.

WAR DIARY INTELLIGENCE SUMMARY.
(Erase heading not required.)

Instructions regarding War Diaries and Intelligence Summaries are contained in F. S. Regs., Part II. and the Staff Manual respectively. Title pages will be prepared in manuscript.

Place	Date	Hour	Summary of Events and Information	Remarks and references to Appendices
	1915			
	Sep 1.		The Battery moved from LAPUGNOY at 3.30 p.m. and arrived at DROUVIN at 5.45 p.m. and bivouaced for the night.	
	2.		The Battery moved from DROUVIN at 7.15 p.m. and arrived at the position originally occupied at LES BREBIS – L.35.D.5.5 – at 10 p.m. the Major line remaining at DROUVIN.	
	3.		Working on gun positions and establishing telephone communication with Observing Station at SOUTH MAROC – M.8.B.8.9.	
	4.		Re-registered guns on original line, & trench at front of DOUBLE CRASSIER – M.4.A.1.3. Registered No.1 gun on PUITS No.16 – M.10.A.5.0.	
	5.			
	6.		The Battery did not fire.	
	7.		A working party was detailed to prepare a new forward position in SOUTH MAROC – M.2.D.8.8. Right Section was registered on Eastern End of DOUBLE CRASSIER – M.5.C.5.0. Left Section was registered on Communt Trench at M.4.D.1.7.	
	8.		Left Section was registered on Communt Trench at M.4.D.9.1. Right Section	

1577 Wt.W10791/1773 500,000 1/15 D. D. & L. A.D.S.S./Forms/C. 2118.

Army Form C. 2118.

Page 2

WAR DIARY
INTELLIGENCE SUMMARY.
(Erase heading not required.)

Instructions regarding War Diaries and Intelligence Summaries are contained in F.S. Regs., Part II. and the Staff Manual respectively. Title pages will be prepared in manuscript.

Place	Date	Hour	Summary of Events and Information	Remarks and references to Appendices
	1915			
	Sep 9		was reported on Enemy's trench at M.10.B.1.5.	
	10		Right Section reported on Enemy's trenches at M.10.A.8.2 and M.10.A.9.3. The Battery did not fire.	
	11		The Right Section fired on targets at M.11.A.3.1 and M.10.D.5.6 with aeroplane observation. No 3 gun fired on DOUBLE CRASSIER. No 1 gun fired at 8.30 pm. on Enemy's transport reported by Infantry at M.10.D.	
	12		No 3 gun reported on front line trench at M.4.C.6.9 and M.4.A.5.0.	
	13		The Battery did not fire.	
	14			
	15		The Battery moved to new forward position in SOUTH MAROC - M.2.D.8.8.	
	16		No 4 gun fired on Enemy's trench.	
	17			
	18		The Battery did not fire.	
	19			
	20			
	21		Bombardment commenced. Battery fired from 8 am to 6 pm according	

1577 Wt.W10791/1773 500,000 1/15 D.D.&L. A.D.S.S./Forms/C. 2118.

Army Form C. 2118.

Page 3

WAR DIARY
INTELLIGENCE SUMMARY
(Erase heading not required.)

Place	Date	Hour	Summary of Events and Information	Remarks and references to Appendices
		19.15	A programme upon the following points in the Enemy's trenches and billets in CITE ST PIERRE — M.11.A.65, M.10.D.5.6, M4.D.3.8-M.5.C.5.0, DOUBLE CRASSIER, South portion of DOUBLE CRASSIER, M.4.C.4.9 through M.4.D.1.3 to East End of DOUBLE CRASSIER to M.4.C.4.9, M.10.A.6.7 – M.10.A.6.7 – M.10.B.2.5, M4.D.1.4 – M.10.A.7.6, M.10.B.0.3, through M4.D.9.3 – M.5.C.5.0 —	
	Sep.22		Bombardment continued. Battery fired on same target as numerous day from 8 a.m. to 6 p.m. according to programme, preceded by two rounds of battery fire on front line trench M.4.A.2.3 – M.4.A.8.7 and one round battery fire on Communication Trench M.5.A.2.6 – G.35.C.6.3. In addition the battery fired on front line trench about M.10.A.5.6 at about 2 p.m.	
	23		Bombardment continued. Battery fired on same target as yesterday from 8 a.m. to 5 p.m. according to programme. In addition, the Battery fired on head of new Communication Trench at M.11.A.2.8 and Entrance to DOUBLE CRASSIER at M.5.C.0.4 and Entrance to Railway Embankment at M.10.B.1.3.	

WAR DIARY

INTELLIGENCE SUMMARY.
(Erase heading not required.)

Place	Date	Hour	Summary of Events and Information	Remarks and references to Appendices
	1915 Sep 24		Bombardment continued. Battery fired on same targets as yesterday according to programme from 8 a.m. till 5.15 p.m. In addition the Battery fired on communication trenches south along the south of the DOUBLE CRASSIER about 2 p.m.	
	25		The Battery opened fire at 5.50 a.m. on the enemy's front line trenches in preparation for the infantry assault at 6.30 a.m. Continued fire throughout the day until about 6 p.m. on front line and communication trenches in zone south of DOUBLE CRASSIER.	
	26		The Battery commenced firing at 9 a.m. a barrage on north of railway on line N.1.A – N.2.A. During the afternoon the Battery fired on the Enemy's works & emplacements on HILL 70 on west side of LENS – LA BASSEE Road.	
	27		Commenced firing at 9.55 a.m. and shelled the copses in M.6.A and fired the same barrage as previous day until 7.35 p.m.	
	28		Fired a few rounds on Enemy's cavalry on LENS – LA BASSEE Road.	
	29		The Battery did not fire.	

Page 5.

WAR DIARY

INTELLIGENCE SUMMARY.

(Erase heading not required.)

Place	Date	Hour	Summary of Events and Information	Remarks and references to Appendices
	1915			
	Sep 30		Fired a few rounds on barge north of railway M.6.D and on cross Roads in CITÉ ST EDOUARD M.6.D.7.2.	

M S Cayzer
Capt. R.F.A. 2/3
for O.C. 22nd London Battery R.F.A.

1.10.15

47TH DIVISION

238 66 E

22ND LONDON BTY R.F.A.
SEP-OCT 1915

WAR DIARY

22ND County of London BTY

Army Form C. 2118.

Instructions regarding War Diaries and Intelligence Summaries are contained in F.S. Regs., Part II. and the Staff Manual respectively. Title pages will be prepared in manuscript.

INTELLIGENCE SUMMARY.

(Erase heading not required.)

Place	Date	Hour	Summary of Events and Information	Remarks and references to Appendices
S. MAROC. M2.D.5.8.	1/10/15		Nothing to record	
	2/10/15		" "	
	3/10/15		Battery fired 157 rounds in Wood VI; 20th Battery also fired on the wood as it was thought to be a strong point in the enemy's new second line in movement.	
	4/10/15		Battery did not fire. Quiet day.	
	5/10/15 1.30PM		Enemy shelled 2. MAROC. Retaliated on Cité St Pierre. 20 rounds fired.	
	6/10/15		20 rounds fired into Cité St Reine in retaliation for shelling of Maroc. Battery ranged on new target Puits 14 Bis. N. end of Wood V. 'E' end of wood V. & S. of Wood V. 16 rounds fired in all.	
	7/10/15		Nothing to record.	
	8/10/15		Information received in the early morning that Germans had delivered an attack in front of Mine Trenches	
		11.30AM	Germans commenced a heavy bombardment of our own trenches the were followed by a counter attack along practically the whole of the line	

Army Form C. 2118.

WAR DIARY

INTELLIGENCE SUMMARY.

(Erase heading not required.)

Instructions regarding War Diaries and Intelligence Summaries are contained in F. S. Regs., Part II. and the Staff Manual respectively. Title pages will be prepared in manuscript.

Place	Date	Hour	Summary of Events and Information	Remarks and references to Appendices
	5/10/15		Retaliation from us on 25th Bgde, we retaliated Scottish failed. Boches were in action all day. Total number of rounds fired 213.	
	9/10/15		45 rounds fired into St Pierre and retaliation to mill. St Maroc.	
	10/10/15		13 rounds fired on enemy front line trench in H19D for experiences purposes. 9 rounds fired into Cité St Pierre in retaliation.	
	11/10		Brisk fire on strafe on shoot length of minnen log on 10/10/15. The enemy failed. Boches fired 432 rounds in retaliation.	
	12/10/15		26 rounds fired in trench in H19D.	
	13/10/15		425 rounds fired in support of attack after Hulluch. Attack failed.	
	14/10/15 15/10/15 16/10/15		Ranging shot and fire.	
	17/10/15		4 rounds fired into Cité St Pierre in retaliation for fire into St Maroc.	
	18/10/15		44 rounds fired on Watch V. 8 rounds fired into St Pierre.	

Army Form C. 2118.

WAR DIARY
~~INTELLIGENCE SUMMARY.~~
(Erase heading not required.)

Instructions regarding War Diaries and Intelligence Summaries are contained in F. S. Regs., Part II. and the Staff Manual respectively. Title pages will be prepared in manuscript.

Place	Date	Hour	Summary of Events and Information	Remarks and references to Appendices
	19/10/15		Remained quiet in Gun Pt Posns	
	20/10/15		The Battery fired 32 rounds on Enemy's trench H.25.B.10.3 to H.19.D.4.D. 12 rounds on Woods N°. 3 and 4. 15 rounds on Wood N°. 6.	
	21.10.15		In the evening the Right Section moved to new position at Foux N°. 7. The Battery fired 32 rounds on Enemy front line trenches.	
	22.10.15		In the evening the Left Section moved to new position at Foux N°. 2. The Battery fired 12 rounds on Cité St. Auguste and repaired on Section on original line.	
	23.10.15		Registered Left section on original line and fired 8 rounds on Cité St. Auguste and Enemy's front line trenches.	
	24.10.15		The Battery fired 8 rounds on Cité St. Auguste and 28 rounds on Enemy's trenches.	
	25.10.15		The Battery fired 56 rounds on Enemy's trenches and 16 rounds on Cité St. Auguste.	
	26.10.15		Registered on section on Redoubt H.20.D & m cabin on Enemy trench. Fired 21 rounds on Enemy trench.	
	27.10.15		Fired 12 rounds on Wood N°. 3. 15 rounds on Cité St. Auguste 17 rounds on trenches.	
	28.10.15		Fired 12 rounds on trenches at 3 and 5 am & 17 rounds during the day.	

Army Form C. 2118.

WAR DIARY
INTELLIGENCE SUMMARY.
(Erase heading not required.)

Place	Date	Hour	Summary of Events and Information	Remarks and references to Appendices
	1915 Oct 29		The Battery fired 93 rounds on enemy's trenches.	
	30		" " 69 " " "	
			" " 8 " " Bois Hugo, and 20 rounds on Hulluch.	
	31		" " 26 " " enemy's trenches, and 10 rounds on Cité St Auguste	

Instructions regarding War Diaries and Intelligence Summaries are contained in F. S. Regs., Part II. and the Staff Manual respectively. Title pages will be prepared in manuscript.

WAR DIARY
or
INTELLIGENCE SUMMARY

Army Form C. 2118.

Vol. 18

Place	Date	Hour	Summary of Events and Information	Remarks and references to Appendices
HAILLICOURT	1/10/15	9am	Walking Exercise. 2827 Lbs (expended) 1387 Tubes (misfires) 293 Plugs, 292 Caps 761 Rings. 300 Cartridge Cases	Afs
HAILLICOURT	2/10/15	9am	returned to D.A.C. Walking Exercise.	Afs
HAILLICOURT	3/10/15	9am	Walking Exercise. Column left HAILLICOURT at 7.30am. Marched along RUE DE LA CITÉ and men billets. 5,7 Tubes (expended) 141 T Tubes (misfires) 42 Plugs, 445 Caps, 155 Spare Rings, 52 Cartridge Cases returned to D.A.C. 23 Cartridges (R.D Cases) issued to D.A.C. and arrived at NOEUX-LES-MINES (LES CORONS) at 6pm.	Afs
NOEUX-LES-MINES	4/10/15	9am	Walking Exercise. 1460 Rds 40lb issued from D.A.C. and issued to 31st Batt. N.Z.	Afs
NOEUX-LES-MINES	5/10/15		200 Rds 50lb received from same Batt. N.Z. Walking Exercise	Afs
NOEUX-LES-MINES	6/10/15	9am	Walking Exercise. 200 7 Tubes received from D.A.C.	Afs
NOEUX-LES-MINES	7/10/15	9am	Walking Exercise. 100 7 Tubes received. 100 7 Tubes issued to 21st Batt N.Z. and 100 7 Tubes issued to 22nd Batt. N.Z.	Afs
NOEUX-LES-MINES	8/10/15	"	368 Rds 50lb received from D.A.C. 926 7 Tubes (expended) 4 7 Tubes (misfires)	Afs
			874 Plugs 865 Caps 30 Rings 738 Cartridge Cases returned to D.A.C.	
NOGON-LES-MINES	9/10/15	9am	Walking Exercise. 200 Rds 50lb issued to 21st Batt. 348 Rds 50lb issued to 22nd Batt N.Z.	Afs
NOEUX-LES-MINES	10/10/15	9am	Walking Exercise. 93 Rds 50lb and 93 Rds 50lb received from D.A.C. and 93 Rds 50lb issued to 21st Battery N.Z.	Afs
			93 Rds 40lb received from D.A.C. 93 Rds 40lb issued to 21st Battery N.Z. 53 Rds 50lb received from D.A.C. 53 Rds 50lb issued to 22nd Battery N.Z.	
NOEUX-LES-MINES	11/10/15	9am	Walking Exercise. 187 Rds 40lb received from D.A.C. 150 Rds 40lb issued to 21st Battery N.Z.	Afs
			returned to D.A.C. :- 169 7 Tubes (expended) 211 7 Tubes (misfires) 368 Plugs 3-5? Caps 44 Rings 192 Cartridge Cases	

Army Form C. 2118.

WAR DIARY
or
INTELLIGENCE SUMMARY.
(Erase heading not required.)

Vol 19

Instructions regarding War Diaries and Intelligence Summaries are contained in F.S. Regs., Part II. and the Staff Manual respectively. Title pages will be prepared in manuscript.

Place	Date	Hour	Summary of Events and Information	Remarks and references to Appendices
NOEUX-LES-MINES	12/10/15	9am	Walking Exercise. 259 Rds 40lb received from D.A.C. 331 Rds 40lb received from D.A.C. 108 Rds 40lb received from D.A.C. 251 Rds 50lb received from 341 Batt W.K. and returned to D.A.C.	do.
NOEUX-LES-MINES	13/10/15	9am	Walking Exercise. 203 Rds 40lb received from D.A.C. 408 Rds 40lb received to 341 Batt W.K. and 221 Rds 40lb received from D.A.C. 5 Shell 50lb received from 22nd Batt W.K. & returned to D.A.C. Returns to D.A.C. :- 934 T Tubes empowered, 745 Plugs 5723 Caps 314 Cartridge Cases.	do.
NOEUX-LES-MINES	14/10/15	9am	Walking Exercise. 264 Rds 40lb received from D.A.C. 760 T Tubes received from D.A.C. 203 Rds 40lb issued to 31st Batt W.K. and 240 Rds 40lb issued to 22nd Batt W.K. 50 Rds 40lb received from D.A.C. 235 Rds 50lb received 14 Shell 9 Cart & 9 Fuzes received from D.A.C & issued to 2nd Batt W.K. Returns to D.A.C. :- 365 T Tubes (ignitors) 244 T Tubes (ignitors) 1306 Plugs 272 Caps 29 Cups 111 Cartridge Cases, 109 Bags Bdcardite from D.A.C.	do.
NIEUX-LES-MINES	15/10/15	9am	Walking Exercise. 505 T Tubes received from D.A.C.	do.
NOEUX-LES-MINES	16/10/15	9am	Walking Exercise.	do.
NOEUX-LES-MINES	17/10/15	9am	Walking Exercise.	do.
		2pm	2 Wagons + 13 men sent on R.B. Fatigue.	
NOEUX-LES-MINES	18/10/15	9am	Walking Exercise. 45 Rds 40lb issued to 2151 Batt W.K. 40 Rds 50lb issued to 22nd Batt W.K. 102 Rds 40lb received from R.A.O. 5 Rds 50lb issued to 22nd Batt W.K. Returns to D.A.O. :- 995 T Tubes empowered, 17 T Tubes misfires, 725 Plugs, 96 Caps, 226 Rings, 1132 Cases.	do.
NOEUX-LES-MINES	19/10/15	9am	Walking Exercise.	do.

1577 Wt.W10791/1773 500,000 1/15 D.D.&L. A.D.S.S./Forms/C. 2118.

WAR DIARY or INTELLIGENCE SUMMARY

Army Form C. 2118.

Vol. 20

Place	Date	Hour	Summary of Events and Information	Remarks and references to Appendices
NOEUX-LES-MINES	20/10/15	9am	Working Exercise. 50 Rds 40lt issued to 21st Bath. M.K. 50 Rds 40lt issued to 22nd Bath. M.K. 11 Rds	a/s
		2pm-4pm	50lt issued to 21st Bath. M.K. Instruction in signalling for 4 N.C.O's	
NOEUX-LES-MINES	21/10/15	9am	Working Exercise. Instruction in signalling for 5 other ranks. 124 Men 40lt received from D.A.O.	a/s
NOEUX-LES-MINES	22/10/15	9am	70 Rds 40lt issued to 21st Bath. M.K. 70 Rds 40lt received from D.A.O. 65 Rds 40lt and 20 Rds 50lt issued to 22nd Bath. M.K. Working Exercise. Instruction in signalling for 4 C/Sgt men. 146 Rds 40lt issued to 21st Bath M.K. 35 Rds 50lt received from 22nd Bath M.K.	a/s
NOEUX-LES-MINES	23/10/15	9am	Working Exercise. 88 Rds 40lt received from D.A.O. 40lt Rds 40lt issued to 22nd Bath M.K. 35 Rds 50lt received from 22nd Bath M.K.	a/s
NOEUX-LES-MINES	24/10/15	9am	Working Exercise. 20 Rds 40lt issued to 21st Bath. M.K. 43 Rds 40lt received from D.A.O.	a/s
NOEUX-LES-MINES	25/10/15	9am	Working Exercise. 64 Rds 40lt issued to 22nd Bath. M.K. 70 Rds 40lt issued to 21st Bath. M.K. 43 Rds 40lt received from D.A.O.	a/s
NOEUX-LES-MINES	26/10/15		43 Rds 40lt issued to 22nd Bath M.K. 60 Rds 40lt received from D.A.O. 40 Rds 40lt issued to 21st Bath M.K. Ups. 146 Rds 40lt received from D.A.O. 20 Can men supplied for Working Party. 461 7 Tubes expended. 886 Plugs. 429 Caps. 82 Rings. 180 Carl. Covers.	a/s
NOEUX-LES-MINES	27/10/15	9am	Working Exercise. 139 Rds 50lt issued to 21st Bath M.K. 62 Rds 40lt issued to 21st Bath M.K. 50 Rds received from D.A.O. 96 Rds 40lt issued to 22nd Bath M.K. 20 N.C.O's men supplied for Working Party.	a/s
NOEUX-LES-MINES	28/10/15	9am	Working Exercise. 20 Rds 40lt received from D.A.O. 145 Rds 40lt issued to 21st Bath M.K. 132 Rds 40lt issued to 22nd Bath M.K. 10 N.C.O's men supplied for Working Party.	a/s
NOEUX-LES-MINES	29/10/15	9am	Working Exercise. 113 Rds 40lt received from D.A.O. 73 Rds 40lt issued to 21st Bath M.K. 40 Rds 40lt issued to 22nd Bath M.K. 10 N.C.O's men supplied for Working Party.	a/s
NOEUX-LES-MINES	30/10/15	9am	Working Exercise. 261 Rds 40lt received from D.A.O. 127 Rds 40lt issued to 21st Bath M.K. 102 Rds 40lt issued to 22nd Bath M.K. 58 Rds 50lt occasioned from D.A.O. 217 Rds 50lt issued to 21st Bath M.K. 10 men supplied for Working Party.	a/s

1577 Wt. W10791/1773 500,000 1/15 D. D. & L. A.D.S.S./Forms/C. 2118.

Army Form C. 2118.

WAR DIARY
or
INTELLIGENCE SUMMARY.
(Erase heading not required.)

Vol 21

Instructions regarding War Diaries and Intelligence Summaries are contained in F. S. Regs., Part II. and the Staff Manual respectively. Title pages will be prepared in manuscript.

Place	Date	Hour	Summary of Events and Information	Remarks and references to Appendices
NOZDI-RESIMES	31/10/15	8pm	Working Evening. 10mm supplied for working party. 9th Row 40th required from 3rd B.C. 91 Rows sold issued to 22nd Batt. M.R. 24 Rows sold & 52 Rows 50lb issued to 31st Batt. Bk.	✓
			Ammunition Summary	
			Receipts & issues for October 1915	
			40lb Shell	
			Received from D.A.O. ... 3,159	
			Issued to Batteries ... 3,147	
			50lb Shell	
			Received from D.A.O. issued to Batteries 765	
			Total issues to date	
			40lb Shell ... 7,342	
			50lb Shell ... 5,077	
			... 12,419	
			[signature] Capt.	

1577 Wt. W10791/1773 500,000 1/15 D.D. & L. A.D.S.S./Forms/C. 2118.

Army Form C. 2118.

WAR DIARY
or
INTELLIGENCE SUMMARY.
(Erase heading not required.)

Vol. 22.

Instructions regarding War Diaries and Intelligence Summaries are contained in F.S. Regs., Part II. and the Staff Manual respectively. Title pages will be prepared in manuscript.

Place	Date	Hour	Summary of Events and Information	Remarks and references to Appendices
NOEUX-LES-MINES	1/11/15	9am	Marching Exercise. 10 men detailed for unloading party. 293 Rev 40lb & 96 Rev 50lb received from D.A.C. 123 Rev 40lb issued to 2/21 Batt. M.T. 19, Rev 40lb issued to 2nd Batt. M.T.	
NOEUX-LES-MINES	2/11/15	9am	Marching Exercise. 45 Rev 40lb received from D.A.C. 15 Rev 50lb issued to 2/21 Batt. M.T. 22 Rev 40lb received 17 Tubes misfires returned D.A.O.	
NOEUX-LES-MINES	3/11/15	9am	Marching Exercise. 52 Rev 40lb & 15 Rev 50lb received from D.A.O. 42 Rev 40lb & 3 Rev 50lb issued to 22nd Batt. M.T. 34 Rev 40lb issued to 22nd Batt. M.T.	
NOEUX-LES-MINES	4/11/15	9am	Marching Exercise. 29 L.D.V.L.R. (Reserve) received at NOEUX-LES-MINES station. 11 (not already included) sent to M.V.S. Total known strength 28. 253 Rev 40lb received from D.A.O. 52 Rev 40lb & 53 Rev 50lb received to 3/21 Batt. M.T. 113 Rev 40lb issued to 22nd Batt. M.T.	
NOEUX-LES-MINES	5/11/15	9am	Marching Exercise. Rumours in camp appt. explosion. 144 Rev 40lb & 202 Rev 50lb received from D.A.C. 20 Rev 40lb & 150 Rev 50lb issued to 3/28 Batt. M.T. 122 Rev 40lb issued to 22nd Batt. M.T.	
NOEUX-LES-MINES	6/11/15	9am	Exercise of Horses. 130 Rev 40lb received from D.A.O. 44 Rev 40lb issued to 2/21 Batt M.T. 150 Rev 40lb received to 22nd Batt. M.T. 210 T. rams misfires returned to D.A.O.	
NOEUX-LES-MINES	7/11/15	9am	Marching Exercise. 144 Rev 40lb & 111 Rev 50lb received from D.A.C. 25 Rev 40lb & 12 Rev 50lb issued to 22nd Batt. M.T. 2/21 Batt. M.T. Signalling for 3 N.C.O.'s men.	
NOEUX-LES-MINES	8/11/15	9am	Marching Exercise. 104 Rev 40lb & 15 Rev 50lb received from D.A.O. 27 Rev 40lb received to 22nd Batt. M.T. Signalling for 3 N.C.O.'s men.	
NOEUX-LES-MINES	9/11/15	9am	Exercise of horses. Signalling for 3 N.C.O. men. 42 Rev 40lb received from D.A.C. 72 Rev 40lb received to 22nd Batt. M.T. 48 Rev 50lb issued to 3/21 Batt. M.T. 52 T. rams (misfires) returned to D.A.O.	
NOEUX-LES-MINES	10/11/15	9am	Marching Exercise. Signalling for 3 N.C.O.'s men. 159 Rev 40lb received from D.A.C. 21 Rev 40lb received horses from D.A.C. 49 Rev 40lb & 27 Rev 50lb issued to 3/25 Batt. M.T. 80 Rev to 80 Rev issued to 22nd Batt. M.T. 4:2 T. rams (exploded) 62 T. rams (misfires) 117 Props 9". Caps 29 Rips 602 Cones	
NOEUX-LES-MINES	11/11/15	9am	Marching Exercise. Signalling for 3 N.C.O.'s men.	
NOEUX-LES-MINES	12/11/15	9am	Marching Exercise. Signalling for 3 N.C.O.'s men. 335 Rev 40lb received from D.A.O. 97 Rev 40lb issued to 2/21 Batt. M.T. 126 Rev 40lb issued to 22nd Batt. M.T. 55 Rev 40lb received to 2/21 Batt. M.T.	
NOEUX-LES-MINES	13/11/15	9am	Marching Exercise. Signalling for 3 N.C.O. men.	
NOEUX-LES-MINES	14/11/15	9am	Marching Exercise. Signalling for 3 N.C.O. men. 16 Cartridges received from D.A.O. 2 Cart. issued 2/22 Batt. M.T.	

1577 Wt. W10791/1773 500,000 1/15 D. D. & L. A.D.S.S./Forms/C. 2118.

Army Form C. 2118.

WAR DIARY
or
INTELLIGENCE SUMMARY.

(Erase heading not required.)

Vol. 23.

Place	Date	Hour	Summary of Events and Information	Remarks and references to Appendices
NOEUX-LES-MINES	15/11/15	9 am	Musketry Exercises. Signalling for SNCO's present.	
NOEUX-LES-MINES	16/11/15	9 am	Column left NOEUX-LES-MINES for FERFAY at 10.40 am travelling via VAUDRICOURT, HESDIGNEUL, LA BUISSIÈRE.	
FERFAY	17/11/15		MARCH and ARCHOL arrived FERFAY 6.40 am. Horses wagons parks arrange new billets. Rough Exercise.	
FERFAY	18/11/15		Musketry Exercises. Wagon parks moved from paddocks south more forward.	
FERFAY	19/11/15		Musketry Exercises. General preparation for inspection by C.O. Bde.	
FERFAY	20/11/15		Genl. Inspection by C.O. Bde. 1 Officer & 2 NCO's attached to D.A.C. for instruction Gunnery r.g.	
FERFAY	21/11/15		Musketry Exercise.	
FERFAY	22/11/15		Musketry Exercise. Received from D.A.C. 629 Rds 2 oll shell.	
FERFAY	23/11/15		Inspection by C.O. Bde in Column of Route at G.11 & G.O. S.T.T. when (moving) Ret. to D.A.C.	
FERFAY	24/11/15		Musketry Exercise. Gun Drill for detachment.	
FERFAY	25/11/15		Skeleton Manoeuvre. Musketry Exercise.	
FERFAY	26/11/15		Preparation for inspection by C.O. Bde.	
FERFAY	27/11/15		General Insp. by C.O. Bde. 31 H.P. horses taken to ZIEGLER ST and 54 L.D. (Remounts) received. Del. Recs Wollaston to 2nd Batt. 150 Rds With received to 2nd Batt.	
FERFAY	28/11/15		Church Parade. Route March.	
FERFAY	29/11/15		Leaving of L.O. Remounts. 16 L.D. (Remounts) exchanged with 16 L.D. from Battery.	

WAR DIARY or INTELLIGENCE SUMMARY.

Army Form C. 2118.

Vol. 24.

Place	Date	Hour	Summary of Events and Information	Remarks and references to Appendices
FERFAY	30/4/15		Coding stocks and general preparations for home leavings.	A.
			Ammunition Summary	
			Receipts issues for November 1915	
			4.5 Howitzer	
			Received from D.A.C.	2379 Rds
			Issued to Batteries	2,063 Rds.
			50 lb Shell	
			Received from D.A.C.	366 Rds
			Issued to Batteries	414 Rds.
			60 lb Shell	9405 Rds A.
			50 lb Shell	5491 Rds
				4896 Rds
			Total Issues to Date:	

47 D40

War Diary of 8th London (Hows) F.A. Brigade

Summary of Information.

Place	Date Hour	
LES BREBIS	Oct. 1st	1915

No 1598- Gunner W.E. PHILLIPS joined 2nd Bar. 9 pm.

2nd Battery returned 96 rounds 4.00 am. to 21st Battery.

2.a. German shells intermittently throughout the day this old front line N and S of LENS - BETHUNE Road. German shelled FOSSE No 7. G.27.C. with 5.9" horizon from 12.45 pm to 1.45 pm. The enemy also shelled LOOS, Western end of DOUBLE CROSSIER, our front line trench South of DOUBLE CROSSIER, FOSSE No 5, and NORTH MAROC, with HE. and shrapnel during the whole of the day.

21st Battery fired 20 rounds and 2nd Battery 104 rounds of 4.5B am. from 22nd Battery.

Batteries and Headquarters waggon-lines formed advanced base at NOEUX LES MINES. Tremendi Recieves and temporaries attackes to Bn. Am Col.

3rd Bn Hos^t. batteries opened fire at 12 noon, the objectives of the 31st Battery being trenches running South from Wood 5 and that of the 2nd Battery being Wood 6. 200 rounds of 4.5 am. were expended by the 31st Battery 4.0 to 6.30 pm - 9.0 pm by 22nd Battery. Between 3pm & 5.30 pm 2nd Battery fired 150 rounds on western by of Wood 6. A. 6.30pm - 9.0 pm Am. Col. formed and waggon lines at NOEUX LES MINES. Event shells South MAROC (Hos & P.U. to Ma P.U.) did incoming shells.

10th (11.50am) A train with 2 locomotives was observed at about H11 A0.6 moving in a EW easterly direction on the WINGLES - PONT-A-VENDIN Railway. About 20 shells mostly shrapnel fell in the vicinity of the works houses in NORTH MAROC between 9 am & 11.30 am. They were possibly from a naval gun first from an armoured train.

Place	Date	Hour	Summary of Information
LES BREBIS	Oct. 4th.		A large amount of transport was observed coming from WINGLES to VENDIN-LE-VIEIL. Parties of marching troops were observed arriving every few minutes on the foot. A large gas flag hoof.
			140 rounds of 4.5" Ho. & 300 Ho. 8.0" Ho. were drawn from our ice once the 40 Ho. an. was close to the starting.
	11.30am		21st Battery fired 7 rounds purposes of bombardment and registration, on trenches east of wood 6 (H31. C.1.5 & H25 a. 0.5.) between 11.30am aug 3.30pm
	3.30pm		At 3.30pm. the bakery fired 20 rounds in retaliation on Cité St PIERRE
	1.45pm		and also fired 10 rounds at 7.45pm on same target. 23rd Siege Battery fired 39 rounds on H25 C.9 (6.5) Rects No 14. bis.
			The Heavy Group of artillery commenced firing at 10.30 am and registered trench systems at H25d (1.5)(6.5). 23rd 22 rounds were fired and several hits were obtained.
			23rd Siege Battery fired at 1.15pm & resorted at 2.30pm when the following points were registered several hits obtained. Houses near H316.(a5)9. 5 rounds were fired on these houses; Corner of trenches N of wood N.S at (2.5)(8.6) on which 10 rounds were fired and several direct hits obtained. Trench S. W. of Puits 14 bis; H. 25. c. 6.5. on which 4 rounds were fired. Sw. edge of wood 4 H.5rd 8. (7.5) on which 12 rounds were fired. A bakery was suspected close to this edge, flashes having been observed.
	3.30 pm.		At 3.30 pm. 22nd Battery fired 5 rounds on Cité St PIERRE in retaliation for enemy shelling of SOUTH MAROC. During the afternoon the battery fired 10 rounds on Cité St PIERRE and the railway embankment between eastern end of DOUBLE CROSSIER and P13. Sharp snap of artillery came out of action.
state presently renounce			
broomstick of impossible.			

LES BREBIS
Point
by Bn

2nd. Bany commenced firing at 2.10 pm and fired 25 rounds on Enemy Snipers
from N.25.d.(1.5)(6) to N.26.d.(9)(7.5). Direct hits were obtained on various points. Fire ceased at 3.15pm.

6y.

2/ov. Bany fired 3 rounds of Battery fire on Cie St LAURENT.

22nd Battery fired 20 rounds on Cie St. LAURENT in retaliation for enemy shelling South MAROC
Wood S and french South hits were registered at 4.30pm.

At 12 noon 23rd Siege Battery fired 88 rounds on N.7a.6.85. (St LAURENT CHURCH)
Only six rounds and spire were visible from the O.P., but a fair aim was obtained
from N. MAROC CHURCH. Several direct hits were obtained on the building. No
wound hit one of the pinnacles of the spire but apparently detonated after
passing through.

7th. 22nd Battery fired 4 rounds in retaliation on Cie St PIERRE. 3rd rounds were
fired on Battery reported in M12.B. light base for aviation observation.

8th. 21st. Battery engaged trenches and redoubt at N.31.c. a.9.4 and N.30.70. The fire
was very effective. During first 3 rounds Germans got out of the trench and ran
across the open to the flank. About 50% of the rounds observed were direct hits
on enemy walls. A barrage was formed from N.1.c.8.8 to N.1.a.8.10.
The whole area of trenches in N.33.c was swept. The total number of
rounds fired was 193.

LES BREBIS.   Cont'd

2no Battery engaged trenches in H.31.b. and N.32.a. The fire was very effective direct hits being obtained. A barrage was formed between H.6.d.9.8 and N.1.c.5.b. The area between M.12.b.10.8 and N.7.a.8.3. in which were several observation & and trenches was thoroughly searched and swept. A barrage was formed between M.6.c.1.5 and M.6.d.6.7. The area M.11 central was searched and swept. A barrage was formed between the following points, M.5.c.7.1. M.5.c.5.0., M.11.a.2.9. H.11.a.2.9. Yalet numbers of barrage fires was 201. The 2no Siege battery engaged trenches at H.25.d.1.6. and H.25.d.2.8. Direct hits were obtained on Church at N.7.a.5.8. which was being used As an Observation Station. Trenches and billets at N.1.d.5.5. were searched and Swept. A very effective fire was directed on to H.31.d.1.5 — Redoubts at Hill 70. — The whole area being swept. Several direct hits were obtained on Puits 14 bis, N.25.a.9.6. The LENS-LABASSEE Road at N.14.a — N.1.a bis Swept. A barrage was formed between N.6.d.3 – N.1.c.5.5. The trenches at H.31.b.3.4 and H.31.b.4.5., the area N.14.a.5.5 to N.8.a.1.1. — Junction of LENS- LABASSEE and BETHUNE Roads. was searched and swept. Redoubts, billets and trenches at H.31.d.5.9 and H.32.c.5.5. were also searched and swept. The total number fired = 154.

Les BRÉBIS

Night
9th.

Between 4.0 pm and 5.35 pm the 22nd Battery fired on the north west front of Cité St. PIERRE using 45, OLE shell.

Between 4.30 pm and 5 pm the vicinity of the 22nd Battery was shelled by very high velocity guns with phosphor shells. At 8.30 pm a considerable number of large H.E. shells fell in front of the battery apparently intended for the communication trench to the railway cutting. The battery fired in retaliation at 9.15 pm. S rounds on Cité St-LAURENT.

LES BREBIS.

8th.
10th. 2.30pm. 22nd Battery registered on Enemy front line trench at H.19.d.4.3 to H.19.a.9.6.
13 rounds were fired and 2 direct hits were made.

4 pm.) 22nd Battery fired retaliatory fire on Enemy battery at H.18.a.5.1. H.18.a.12.1.
(H.18.c.12.8½.

3pm. 21st. Battery fired on Enemy trench H.19.c.8.0 to H.19.c.9.6. This trench was not finally registered. 9 rounds were fired & 3 direct hits were seen.

4 pm. Battery fired in retaliation on Enemy battery M.11.b.8.5½ and M.12.a.3.3.

1.50 pm. 23rd Siege Battery fired 9 rounds and registered on special point on LENS - LA BASSEE Road at H.19.a.7.8. and H.13.d.35.9½. 6 rounds were fired on road at H.13.d.35.9½. which were forwarded.

4.10 pm. Battery fired in retaliation on Enemy battery at N.1.a.4.5.

11th. 6.15pm from 6.15pm to 10.15pm. 22nd Battery fired by rounds on Eastern end of BREBIS. and Railway running South West for 200 yards.

2pm. to 3.30pm 21st. Battery fired 114 rounds on enemy trenches along railway at M.6.c.4.6½ to M.5.a.2.3. 3.30 pm 27 rounds were fired on an Enemy battery at M.6.b.8½. 9. and at 4 pm 6 rounds were fired on enemy trenches along Railway. At 4 pm to 4.10pm 21 rounds were fired on these trenches. From 4.2 pm to 4.15pm. At 4.15pm 59 rounds were fired on enemy trenches in Cite St. Pierre and again at this trenches.

LES BREBIS

Oct.
11th. 2pm. 2 Siege Battery fired on enemy trenches along railway – M.12.a.s.6. to M.12.a.9.8½.
and also on trenches between railway at M.6.c.3.5. to M.6.c.5.4.

2.43pm. Battery fired on enemy trenches at M.6.c.5.1 to M.7.c.7.3.

3.19 pm. The area between #N.1.c and N.7.a. was searched and swept.

4.35pm. Battery fired on enemy trench at M.6.c.4.4. to M.6.a.8.0.

2pm – 2.45pm 22nd Battery fired 101 rounds on trench along railway at M.5:c.9.2½.
and on trenches and billets on Cité St PIERRE at M.11.a and M.11.b.

2.47pm 9 rounds were fired on enemy battery positions at H.R. L.S.I.

2.50pm – 2.55pm. The enemy trench along railway and trenches and billets in
Cité St PIERRE were again fired on 10 rounds being expended.

2.55 – 3pm. 1 Drummer was fired on communication trench running south
at Eastern line of DOUBLE CROSSIER including line to 11.

3pm – 3.8pm. Trench along Railway and trenches and billets at Cité St PIERRE
were again fired on, 16 rounds being expended.

3.8pm. 8 rounds were fired on enemy battery.

3.10 pm. Trench along Railway at M.5.c.9.2½ and trenches and billets in Cité St. PIERRE
were fired on 140 rounds being expended.

4.41. pm. 31 rounds were fired on Railway from M.5.c.4.2. to M.5.a.7.4.

6.3 pm. Enemies batteries in M.10.6.2.3. and M.10.a.8.1. were fired on 20 rounds being
expended.

LES BREBIS.	Dec. 11. 5.50pm	9 rounds were fired on enemys batteries in the area M.8.a.2.8, 4.9, 7.9, 6.6.
	6.5 pm.	French dud South from Eastern end of DOUBLE CRASSIER and enemy batteries at M.10.b.2.8 and M.10.b.8.
	6.15 pm.	From 6.15 pm to 10.15 pm, 3 rounds being fired on, 5 rounds being registered of DOUBLE CRASSIER and railway running South East for 250 yards. From 6.15 pm to 10.15 pm. 69 rounds were fired on the Eastern end 2/Lieut. J. Caulfield Stokes and L.A.B. Stephenson with 15 O.R's from 9th London (Rons) Val Bn. arrived from the Base. Brigade Headquarters and each batteries had 5 men each attached to them while Lt. J. Caulfield Stokes was attached to the 2/S. Battery and L/G.A.B. Stephenson was attached to 92nd Battery.
	12th.	
	At 4.3 pm	3 rounds were fired on Ais St PIERRE. A fire was started in Ais St PIERRE.
	6.30 pm	French H.Q.a.3.2. At 8.30 pm. battery fired 18 rounds on Ais St PIERRE and railway. 22nd battery fired on and registered enemy's from their trench at H.Q.a.0.5.2. 4 guns registered and 26 rounds were expended. Registration carried at M.I.I.C.Y.6. M.11.C.6.6.
	4.15 pm.	to H.Q.a.0.5.2.
	5.15pm	At 5.15 pm. 22nd battery fired one salvo on M.10.a.6.6. M.11.a.3.1.

LES BREBIS.	Oct. 12.	2pm.	23rd Siege Battery registered three rounds LENS LABASSEE Road at H.13.c.85.2. Target was visible from LOOS and HAYDC church. 5 rounds were fired.
	13th.	12.30pm.	21st. Battery fired 117 rounds. on German front line trench at H.19.a.1.8 to H.19.a.8.1.
		2 pm	At 2 pm. 143 rounds were fired also on trenches and houses 3, 4 and 5. At 3.40 pm 26 rounds were fired on the same place. From 4.46 pm to 5 pm. 25 rounds were fired on German front line trench at H.19.a.1.8 to H.19.a.8.1. Three guns only were in action, and during the first period two only for some time, owing to three broken dragshoe chains.
		12.30 pm.	164 rounds were fired by 22nd Battery on German front line trench at H.19.a.25.3 - H.19.a.8.0.
		2 pm	From 2 pm. to 5.8 pm. 232 rounds were fired on H.19.a.25.0.16 H.19.a.2.3. from 5.8 pm to 6.5 pm a barrage was formed between H.19.c.8.8 to H.19.a.0.5. 29 rounds being fired.
		12.50 pm.	23rd Siege Battery opened fire on German front line trench and houses at H.19.a.8.0. to H.13.c.8.2. and H.19.a.8.6 to H.13.c.4.2.
		2 pm.	170 rounds were fired on WESTERN edge of HAILLUCH – H.13.a.3.6 to H.13.c.2.15.
		2.13 pm.	35 rounds was fired into HAILLOCH – H.13.6.7.05 to H.13.6.4.5. At 2.30 pm fire was directed on another point in AILLUCH – H.14.a.1.7. and H.13.6.6.6 on which 73 rounds were expended and again at 3.30 pm to H.13.d.3.6. to H.13.6.2.1. on which 150 rounds were expended.
	14th.		

LES BREBIS Oct 2/1 Battery fired 4 rotations rounds at 5pm on fete de PIERRE in retaliation for shelling N.17.a.o.c.
22nd/15 19th 12 rounds on the BOIS H.26.9.0 Trenches. At 7.30 pm 12 rounds were again fired into
Cie S.PIERRE in retaliation

22nd Battery fired 6 rounds into Cie St. Pierre in retaliation for shelling S.17.A.9.o.c.
At 5.30pm. Heavy rifle & M.G. fire was heard in direction of HOHENZOLLERN Redoubt.
Between 3pm & 3.7 pm. 23rd Siege Battery fired 24 rounds on H.14.c.3.3. Too much fog
to observe effect. At 5.38 pm. 10 rounds were fired on H.25.c.2.65. and H.25.c.1.75.

6 rounds fired at 10.49 pm. on H.33.c.5.2. Cie St AUGUSTE
30.th 21st/4th Battery engaged enemy trench H.19.a.4.0. H.25. 6.10.3 at 12 noon
an 24st Each battery fired
an avoided. 32 rounds being experienced at 1.15 pm. very effectively
12 rounds into WOOD 3 and 5 of WOOD 4. Enemy trenches in
Woods 4 and 5 were engaged at 4 pm. 30 rounds being exchanged.
At 12 noon At 4 pm. 22nd Battery searched WOOD 6, expending 15 rounds.
At 2.50 pm. 23rd Siege Battery fired on Railway at H.25.d.1.6. H.26.c.4.8 on
report that Germans were massing near Bois H650.
At 4 pm. 23rd Battery fired 20 rounds on PUITS 14 bis & WOOD 3.

LES BREBIS. Oct. 21st.

At 2 p.m. 16 rounds ~~Lewis~~ each Battery fires on German front line trench at H.19.a.8.0. to H.19.a.6.5. this was repeated at 2.20 pm. At 2.20 pm 21st Battery engaged German gun-pits first and afterwards 2.40pm German pits opposing bivouacs.

The right section 8 22nd Battery having moved to FOSSE 7, registered Pits re his At 3.34 pm. 23rd Siege battery dispatched and ranged on pits N.3.a.6.6. 8 rounds being expended.

22nd.
At 12.23 pm. 21st Bany. fired 17 rounds on bivouacs 4 + 5 in retaliation for Germans shelling Chalk Pits. At 1.39 pm. shelled LOOS. — The 21st Bany retaliated by firing 8 rounds into Cite St AUGUSTE and the 28th Siege battery retaliated by firing 8 rounds on H.33.6.7.3 and N.33.a.4.6.
At 4 pm Germans shelled Whole British front line. The 21st ~~and 23rd~~ Battalion retaliated by shelling Cite St. AUGUSTE. 12 + 16 rounds being expended respectively. The 23rd Siege battery retaliated by firing 8 rounds on H.13.6.42.0. The 40th battery R.F.A. came into the Huy Group at 10 am. They registered on Pits 13bis, Cross roads at H.13.a. and a house at H.13.a.2.5. At 12.30 pm battery retaliated on BOIS HUGO for German bombing Chalk Pits. At 4 pm. battery retaliated on Cite St. AUGUSTE and HULLUCH for Germans shelling British front line. 23rd Siege battery fired 14 rounds in retaliation for shelling Chalk Pits. on N.33.a.4.6. and N.33.a.62.65.

Oct.
LES BRŒ BIS. 22.

22. Battery Departures on Puits 11 to his experiencing 26 rounds at 12.30 pm. Battery fired 13 rounds in retaliation at 4.20 a.m in retaliation for shelling; Chalk Pits.
Lt Col Erskey left for England on 7 days leave, Major Rea, 4th Battery assumed command of Erskey Group during his absence.

23. At 10.40 p 31st Battery fired 20 rounds on site de Angluste in retaliation for German shelling Chalk Pits.
At 3.40 p 22nd Battery fired 1 round at FERME DES MINES in retaliation for German shelling and 2 rounds at 4.27.c.3.0 and 2 rounds at 26.d.3.4.
Puits 11 Sud was registered until 15 rounds at 4.15 pm

At 11 am 31st Battery fired on track 4.7.a.2.3. to 4.7.a.4.9 and Searched back for 100 yards. This was repeated at 11.20 am & the second line fired on 4.1.b. to 4.2 was registered.
Lt: I.R. Henderson joined here from 1st Seige Battery at Erskey Group.
2nd Seige Battery left Erskey Group.

2½ Bde R.F.A. Bde

Oct 21st /22nd Battery/ 21st Battery in reply to enemy shelling LOOS and our support trench, 8 rounds on our support trench.
For German shelling LOOS and our support trench, 10 rounds were fired on N.33.a.4.5 in retaliation for enemy shelling our front line trenches on N.25.b.4.8 and trenches from N.25.b.5.0 to N.25.b.7.7.

At 1 pm 21st Battery fired 25 rounds on trenches N.25.b.4.8 and trenches from N.25.b.5.0 to N.25.b.7.7 in retaliation for Germans shelling our trenches.

At 2.30 pm 40th Battery fired 20 rounds on trenches in retaliation for enemy shelling LOOS and support trenches. At 3.10 pm battery fired 5 rounds on trenches in retaliation for Germans shelling our trenches near C.M.b.9.5. from trench N.19.2.4.5

At 4 pm battery fired 4 rounds per gun retaliation on trench N.19.2.4.1 to N.19.d.70 in retaliation for Germans shelling our trenches.

After the 4 pm bombardment, the enemy retaliation slightly on LOOS and CHALK PIT WOOD.

22nd At 11 am each battery bombarded enemy's second line trench from N.13.b.1.2 to N.13.a.9.2 with 2 rounds per gun. At 11.10 am this was repeated and again at 11.20 am when 4 rounds per gun were fired in return.

At 11.10 pm 21st & 40th batteries fired on the trenches, in retaliation for enemy shelling CHALK PIT. At the same time 22nd battery fired 16 rounds on C to L August in retaliation for German shelling LOOS with an 8.7 howitzer. About three rounds as a 30pm the Battery fired 8 rounds in retaliation for German shelling LOOS & British front line trenches.

LES BREBIS (cont.)
26. Germans shelled upon our trenches from Chalk Pit Wood with light field gun
fire the vicinity between LES BREBIS VERMELLES with howitzer guns.
All three batteries retaliated at different intervals during the day on
Au S. LAURENT, Au S. AUGUSTE AND WOODS V.5.Y.8

27. Major Bell, Brevet Rank Major S'Elin assumed command of The Group.
During the morning 21st Battery 26 rounds on BOIS Hr.90 and Cité St LAURENT
in retaliation for the Germans shelling LOOS and our trenches
at 12.21. German shelled LOOS. 21st Battery retaliated with 16 rounds
on Cité St AUGUSTE. Germans shelled our front line trenches during
the afternoon for which we retaliated by shelling their
trenches round Wood 6. LOOS was again shelled at 3pm.
Retaliation was carried out on Cité St LAURENT.

28. At 9. am Germans shelled our front line trenches. We
retaliated on German trenches Notch and south of PRITS 14 & 6½.
An Observation Station having been located at H.32.a.6.2. 12 rounds
were fired into it by Hot Battery. During the afternoon the
Hot Battery fired 14 rounds on O.S. at H.31.b.6.0 and the trenches
close by it, in retaliation for Germans shelling our front line
trenches. At 4.30 pm Germans fired 11 rounds of 5.9 shell at MARoc Church.

LES BREBIS.   Oct. 29.

At 10.31 am, 21st Battn fired on 8 rounds each on C/o & PIERRE and H.26.a.0.3. in retaliation for German shelling CHALK PIT.

At 12.42 pm. 21st battery fired 22rounds on H.31.b.3.0. in retaliation for German shelling our front line trenches and again at 2.10 pm. 12 rounds were fired on H.31.b.3.5. to H.31.b.2.10. for the same good. At 3 pm. enemy shelled CHALK PIT and our front line trenches. The ELEY GROUP retaliated by a slow bombardment on WOOD, trenches at H.19.d.2.3, HULLUCH and on PUITS 14 bis.

Some movement observed by an Bleuer

Oct. 30.

Lt. Col. E.H.ELEY returned from leave & took over command of ELEY GROUP.

At 9 am 21st Battery retaliated on BOIS HUGO with 4 rounds for enemy shelling our front line trenches. During the greater part of the morning the Germans shelled our trenches, the Eley Group retaliating on BOIS HUGO, C/o de PIERRE and PUITS 14 bis. During the afternoon the enemy shelled the CHALK PIT and WOOD the Eley Group retaliated on fire at LAURENT and the trenches round trench 6 and H.19.

At 3 pm ELEY Group slowly bombarded German lines at SLOPE.

21st Battery. 16 rounds on trenches H.19.A.5.2 to H.19.b.10.6
9da Battery 16 rounds on trench H.19.a.9.4
40th Battery 24 rounds on trenches H.19.a and b.

From 10 am to 11 am and from 2.30 pm to 3.30 pm German shelled seend of forest with heavy H.E. shell.

LES BREBIS Oct
          21st

During the whole day, the German shelling LOOS and our front line trenches. Retaliation was carried out as follows:-

At 10.34 am 2nd Battery fired 4 rounds on LIE à IMPERIAL in retaliation for enemy shelling LOOS. At 12.31 Battery fires 4 rounds of shrapnel on Kench's in retaliation for German shelling our front line trench.

At 12.29 pm 4 rounds were fired on CITE S PIERRE in retaliation for Germans shelling LOOS. Then was repeated on CITE S LAURENT at 12.38 pm for the same reason.

At 12.50 pm battery again engaged the German front line trench W of Wood 6 firing 8 rounds in retaliation for German shelling our front line trenches.

At 1.30 pm 21st Battery fires 12 rounds into CITE S LAURENT and the 2nd Battery 4 rounds on H.26.a.0.8. in retaliation for German shelling LOOS.

At 1.35 pm 22nd Battery fires 4 rounds on H.19.a.9.0 in retaliation for German shelling our trenches. During the rest of the afternoon retaliation was carried out on CITE S LAURENT, CITE S PIERRE and fires 14 hrs for enemy shelling of LOOS and our trenches.

47th Division

1/8th London (How) Bde R.F.A.

Nom.
Vol IX

12/7663

Army Form C. 2118

WAR DIARY
or
INTELLIGENCE SUMMARY.
(Erase heading not required.)

Instructions regarding War Diaries and Intelligence Summaries are contained in F. S. Regs., Part II. and the Staff Manual respectively. Title pages will be prepared in manuscript.

Place	Date	Hour	Summary of Events and Information	Remarks and references to Appendices
LES BREBIS L.35.a.6.7. Sheet 36b. 1/40,000	Nov. 1st.		During the whole day Germans shelled LOOS and CHALK PIT WOOD considerably. Retaliation was carried out by both batteries on CITES ST LAURENT, ST PIERRE and ST AUGUSTE, BOIS HUGO and German front trenches. 21st Battery fired 69 rounds in retaliation and 22nd Battery 50 rounds. At 6 p.m. and 6.30 p.m. both batteries fired 16 rounds on WOOD 6 for purposes of bombardment.	
	2nd.		Germans again shelled LOOS and front line trenches. Retaliation was carried out by both batteries - 22nd Battery firing 24 rounds on PUITS 14 bis and trench at H.19.d.4.0. and 21st Battery fired 26 rounds on trench W. of WOOD 6.	
		4.30p.m. 6.45p.m.	Both batteries fired 8 rounds on German trenches as part of the scheme of bombardment. This was repeated.	
	3rd	6 am.	As part of the bombardment scheme adopted by the ELEY GROUP, 16 rounds were fired by both batteries at 6 a.m. on trench H.14.c.9.3. to H.20.b.2.9. and H.13.c.2.4. to H.14.c.0.5½. During the morning LOOS and front trenches were shelled. Retaliation was carried out by both batteries on CITE ST LAURENT, trenches W. of WOOD 6, PUITS 14 bis and H.26.a.0.3. 21st Battery fired 44 rounds in retaliation and 22nd Battery 89 rounds. Lt. R.G.TOMLINSON and Capt. J.F.SMITH (R.A.M.C.) with 3 oth r ranks granted 9 days leave of absence to ENGLAND. Capt. T.J.FAULKNER (R.A.M.C.) of the 5th London F.A.B. took over the duties of Medical Officer to the Brigade.	
	4th		ELEY GROUP adopted a scheme of bombardment by which each battery had a certain section of the line allotted to it. Each battery was to bombard that section with 17 rounds per gun up to 5 p.m. and give 3 salvoes during the night making the expenditure 20 rounds per gun. All retaliation on enemy shelling CHALK PIT WOOD was carried out by 22nd Battery and 40th Battery on Northern half of CITE ST AUGUSTE. Retaliation by 21st Battery was directed onto billets and trenches in CITES ST PIERRE and ST EDOUARD.	
		1a.m.	From 11 a.m. to 5 p.m. both batteries fired 68 rounds on their allotted portion of the line viz:- 21st Battery, trenches West of WOOD 6 - from H.25.c.6.6. - H.31.b.1.7. and the 22nd Battery junction of trenches at H.19.a.4.0. to H.26.a.0.3½. During the afternoon the Germans shelled LOOS and CHALK PIT WOOD. Retaliation was carried out on CITES ST AUGUSTE, ST PIERRE and ST LAURENT by both batteries.	
	5th		Bombardment was carried out on the same points as yesterday, the same number of rounds being	

Army Form C. 2118.

WAR DIARY
or
INTELLIGENCE SUMMARY.
(Erase heading not required.)

Instructions regarding War Diaries and Intelligence Summaries are contained in F.S. Regs., Part II. and the Staff Manual respectively. Title pages will be prepared in manuscript.

Place	Date	Hour	Summary of Events and Information	Remarks and references to Appendices
LES BREBIS L.35.c.6.7. Sheet 36b. 1/40,000	Nov. 1st.		During the whole day Germans shelled LOOS and CHALK PIT WOOD considerably. Retaliation was carried out by both batteries on CITES ST LAURENT, ST PIERRE and ST AUGUSTE, BOIS HUGO and German front trenches. 21st Battery fired 69 rounds in retaliation and 22nd Battery 50 rounds.	
		6 pm.	At 6 p.m. and 6.30 p.m. both batteries fired 16 rounds on WOOD 6 for purposes of bombardment.	
	2nd.		Germans again shelled LOOS and front line trenches. Retaliation was carried out by both batteries - 22nd Battery firing 24 rounds on PUITS 14 bis and trench at H.19.d.4.0. and 21st Battery fired 26 rounds on trench W. of WOOD 6.	
		4.30 p.m.	Both batteries fired 8 rounds on German trenches as part of the scheme of bombardment.	
		6.45 p.m.	This was repeated.	
	3rd	6 am	As part of the bombardment scheme adopted by the ELEY GROUP, 16 rounds were fired by both batteries at 6 a.m. on trench H.14.c.9.3. to H.20.b.2.9. and H.13.c.2.4. to H.14.c.0.3. During the morning LOOS and front trenches were shelled. Retaliation was carried out by both batteries on CITE ST LAURENT, trenches W. of WOOD 6, PUITS 14 bis and H.26.a.0.3. 21st Battery fired 44 rounds in retaliation and 22nd Battery 89 rounds. Lt. R.G.TOMLINSON and Capt. J.F.SMITH (R.A.M.C.) with 3 other ranks granted 9 days leave of absence to ENGLAND. Capt. T.J.FAULKNER (R.A.M.C.) of the 5th London F.A.B. took over the duties of Medical Officer to the Brigade.	
	4th		ELEY GROUP adopted a scheme of bombardment by which each battery had a certain section of the line allotted to it. Each battery was to bombard that section with 17 rounds per gun up to 5 p.m. and give 3 salvoes during the night making the expenditure 20 rounds per gun. All retaliation on enemy shelling CHALK PIT WOOD was carried out by 22nd Battery and 40th Battery on Northern half of CITE ST AUGUSTE. Retaliation by 21st Battery was directed onto billets and trenches in CITES ST PIERRE and ST EDOUARD.	
		1 a.m.	From 11 a.m. to 5 p.m. both batteries fired 68 rounds on their allotted portion of the line viz:- 21st Battery, trenches West of WOOD 6 - from H.25.c.6.6. - H.31.b.1.7. and the 22nd Battery junction of trenches at H.19.a.4.0. to H.26.a.0.3. During the afternoon the Germans shelled LOOS and CHALK PIT WOOD. Retaliation was carried out on CITES ST AUGUSTE, ST PIERRE and ST LAURENT by both batteries.	

Bombardment was carried out on the same points as yesterday, the same number of rounds being

WAR DIARY
or
INTELLIGENCE SUMMARY

(Erase heading not required.)

Army Form C. 21

Instructions regarding War Diaries and Intelligence Summaries are contained in F.S. Regs., Part II. and the Staff Manual respectively. Title pages will be prepared in manuscript.

Place	Date	Hour	Summary of Events and Information	Remarks and references to Appendices
LES BREBIS	Nov. 5th		Bombardment was carried out on the same points as yesterday, the same number of rounds being fired. LOOS and our front line trenches were shelled - retaliation being carried out by both batteries. From 1 p.m. to 3.30 p.m. 22nd Battery fired 80 rounds in retaliation on trench H.25.b.central to H.26.d.3.0. and on H.26.d.2½.0.	
	6th		During the greater part of the afternoon, German artillery was fairly active and LOOS and FOSSE 7 were shelled. Retaliation on CITE ST LAURENT, FOSSE 12 and an O.S. near FOSSE 12, was carried out by both batteries, 21st Battery firing 28 rounds and 22nd Battery 20 rounds. Bombardment was also carried out on the same targets as yesterday, salvoes being fired at 9.15 p.m., 9.45 p.m. and 11.30 p.m.	
	7th	2.30p.m.	Bombardment carried out on trench H.13.d.2.6. to H.13.d.5.5. At 4 p.m. 8 rounds were fired by Battery on that target. After this short bombardment the enemy retaliated with a large number of H.E. shell just South of FOSSE 7. Capt. H.J.McVEAGH joined the Brigade from ENGLAND and was posted to 22nd Battery supernumerary to establishment.	
	8th		Germans shelled our support trenches during the morning. Retaliation was carried out on CITE ST PIERRE and on German trenches round HULLUCH and from H.30.b.central to H.26.d.2½.0. At 9.10 p.m. and 10 p.m. All batteries of ELEY GROUP bombarded enemy trench H.13.d.2.5. to H.13.d.8.5. firing two salvoes. This was repeated at 9.10 p.m. and 10 p.m. At 3 p.m. the enemy shelled the eastern side of FOSSE 7 with heavy H.E. shells. A class for the training of 3 N.C.Os. and men was started in the Brigade Ammunition Column.	
	9th	1 pm	Germans shelled LOOS and CHALK PIT during the whole of the day. Retaliation was carried out by both batteries. 21st Battery fired 30 rounds on CITE ST LAURENT between 10 a.m. and 12.30 p.m. 12 rounds on trenches West of WOOD 6 at 3.49 p.m. and 1 round on trench in WOODS 4 & 5. 22nd Battery fired 4 rounds on enemy trench H.32.b.central to H.26.d.2½.0. at 1 p.m. and 1.10 p.m. 8 rounds on same target in retaliation. Bombardments were carried out as follows :- At 1 p.m. both batteries fired 2 salvoes on trenches H.25.b.3.7. - H.25.b.10.3. and at 7 p.m., 7.20 p.m. and 7.50 p.m. 8 rounds were fired each time by both batteries on tracks running from H.20.c.4.8. to H.20.a.5.1.	

Army Form C. 2118

WAR DIARY
or
INTELLIGENCE SUMMARY.
(Erase heading not required.)

Instructions regarding War Diaries and Intelligence Summaries are contained in F. S. Regs., Part II. and the Staff Manual respectively. Title pages will be prepared in manuscript.

Place	Date	Hour	Summary of Events and Information	Remarks and references to Appendices
LES BREBIS	10th	2 p.m.	Bombardment commenced at 2 p.m. with the 21st Battery firing 2 salvoes on Southern portion of WOOD 6 and 22nd Battery firing 2 salvoes on Western end of WOOD 6.	
		3 p.m.	Both batteries fired 3 salvoes on Redoubt in H.20.d.central. At 9 p.m. both batteries fired 2 salvoes each on trenches from H.20.c.4.6. to H.20 central. LOOS, CHALK PIT WOOD and our front line trenches were shelled by the enemy. Both batteries carried out retaliation on WOODS 4-5 & 6. CITE ST PIERRE and enemy's front line trenches.	
	11th	5.55 a.m.	Fire opened at 5.55 a.m. by both batteries firing 2 salvoes each on enemy's trenches, 21st Battery taking trenches from H.26.a.0.5½. to H.20.d.1.1. and 22nd Battery H.19.b.4.9. to H.14.c.2.3. This was repeated at 6.15 a.m. LOOS and our front line trenches were shelled and our batteries retaliated on enemy trenches round PUITS 14 bis, CITE ST LAURENT and on the LENS-BETHUNE Road.	
		4.50 p.m.	Both batteries fired 8 rounds in bombardment on trenches H.26.a.9.9. to H.20.c.6.5.	
	12th	8 a.m.	Bombardment opened by both batteries firing three salvoes each on PUITS 14 bis and again at 8.20 a.m.	
		5.30 p.m.	21st Battery fired two salvoes on trenches from H.13.d.3.6. to H.13.b.8.2. and the 22nd battery fired 2 salvoes on H.13.b.4.0. to H.14.a.0.7. Both batteries repeated this at 5.45 p.m. and 6.20 p.m.	
			Germans shelled CHALK PIT about noon and 21st Battery retaliated by firing 12 rounds on trench W. of WOOD 6. At 4 p.m. 22nd Battery fired 4 rounds on PUITS 14 bis in retaliation for enemy shelling our front line trenches.	
	13th	9 a.m.	Fire opened with a slow bombardment for one hour of 6 rounds per gun by each battery. The objective of the 21st Battery was a line from H.25.b.9.5. to H.26.a.1.2. and that of 22nd Battery H.26.a.1.2. to H.26.c.0.9.	
		2.50 p.m.	At 2.50 p.m. and 3 p.m. 2 rounds per gun were fired in salvoes by both batteries on trench along W. edge of WOOD 3 and WOOD 4. Enemy shelled CHALK PIT WOOD during the afternoon and both batteries retaliated.	
	14th	5.45 a.m.	At 5.45 and 6.5 a.m. 2 rounds per gun were fired in salvoes on trench.s H.19.b.8.4. to H.20.c.4.8. and H.19.b.4.0. to H.19.b.4.9. Both batteries fired 2 rounds per gun in salvoes on H.13.d.2.10. to H.13.d.2.5. During the afternoon the Germans shelled LOOS, MAROC and our front line trenches very heavily. Retaliation was carried out by both batteries on CITE ST LAURENT, FOSSE 12 and enemy front line trenches. 21st battery firing 34 rounds and 22nd Battery 20 rounds.	1

Army Form C. 2118

WAR DIARY
or
INTELLIGENCE SUMMARY
(Erase heading not required.)

Instructions regarding War Diaries and Intelligence Summaries are contained in F. S. Regs., Part II. and the Staff Manual respectively. Title pages will be prepared in manuscript.

Place	Date	Hour	Summary of Events and Information	Remarks and references to Appendices
LES BREBIS	15th	5.15 a.m.	Fire opened at 5.15 a.m. when both batteries fired 2 salvoes each on enemy trenches at M.13.d.2.10. to M.13.d.2.5. This was repeated at 6.10 a.m.	
		12.50 p.m.	21st Battery fired 25 rounds on trench W. of WOOD 6 in retaliation for enemy shelling CHALK PIT. One bomb proof shelter was destroyed.	
		12.40 p.m.	22nd Battery fired 24 rounds on M.32.b.central to M.26.d.2.0. in bombardment and at 1.35 p.m. fired 8 rounds on a trench S. of PUITS 14 bis in retaliation for enemy shelling trenches in vicinity of CHALK PIT COPSE. At 2.10 p.m. 22nd battery fired 4 rounds on same target for the same reason.	
		2.19 p.m.	21st battery engaged an enemy battery at M.11.a.3.2. firing 12 rounds and causing much damage.	
	15th	3.30 p.m.	21st Battery 12 rounds on Railway and trench at M.5.d.5.4. to M.6.c.3.7. in retaliation for enemy shelling our front line trenches. Much damage was done to Railways and 4 rounds burst in the trenches.	
			During the night 1 section of each Battery moved out of position into rest at FERFAY.	
		10.5 a.m.	21st Battery fired 21 rounds on enemy batteries in WOOD 6 in retaliation for enemy shelling CHALK PIT WOOD.	
			During the night Brigade Headquarters, the remaining sections of 21st and 22nd Batteries and Brigade Ammunition Column moved from their positions and went into rest at FERFAY.	
FERFAY	17th		Lt. K. HARDING joined the Brigade and was attached to Brigade Ammunition Column. The Brigade spent the day in putting up horse lines, taking over billets, &c. The following Officers & N.C.Os. & men were attached for a 12 days course in telephony to the 47th Divisional Signal Co. at MARLES-LES-MINES:- Lt. CAULFEILD STOKER, 21st Battery, 866 Gr. FURZE, Bde.H.Qs. 441 Br. EDWARDS and 851 Gr. McCARTNEY 21st Battery, 1543 Gr. CUNNINGHAM 22nd Battery, 977 Gr. BROWN and Capt. F. de WITT and Capt. LARGEN and 13 other ranks left for ENGLAND via HAVRE on 9 days leave.	
	18th		The Brigade improved their lines, cleaned harness and equipment. The overhauling of the guns of the 21st Battery was commenced under Ordnance Artificer.	
	19th		The Brigade improved their lines, cleaned harness and equipment.	
	20th		The O.C. Brigade inspected the lines, harness and equipment. The following Officers and N.C.Os. proceeded on a course of Gunnery, Battery tactics, Ammunition supply and Horse management at	

Army Form C. 2118

WAR DIARY
or
INTELLIGENCE SUMMARY.

(Erase heading not required.)

Instructions regarding War Diaries and Intelligence Summaries are contained in F.S. Regs., Part II. and the Staff Manual respectively. Title pages will be prepared in manuscript.

Place	Date	Hour	Summary of Events and Information	Remarks and references to Appendices
FERFAY	20th		47th Divisional Ammunition Column:- Lt. HENDERSON, 2/Lt. STEPHENSON, 2/Lt. LAWTHER, No.818 Cpl. MOODY, No.996 Br. BYRON, No.755 Cpl. WATT, No.308 Cpl. SAYERS No.371 Sgt. CARTER, No.634 Cpl. TILLOTSON, No.1131 @/Br. FERMOR, No.723 @/Br. GILLARD.	
	21st		Divine Service was held in the School Room.	
	22nd		Gun drill and riding drill was carried out. Lt. TOMLINSON returned from leave.	
	23rd		The Brigade was inspected in Drill Order by the O.C. and a Route March was afterwards carried out. Lt. HARDING was attached to the 47th Divisional Ammunition Column for duty.	
	24th		Battery training carried out. Capt. COWAN, Lt. KINDELL and 13 other ranks granted 9 days leave to ENGLAND.	
	25th	2 pm	The Brigade carried out Tactical Exercises in Skeleton Order. Instruction in Signalling was given by Sgt. HENLEY to all Signallers. A detachment of men from Brigade Ammunition Column practiced Gun Drill. The remainder of the Brigade were on harness cleaning and a general overhaul.	
	26th		150 men N.C.Os. and men bathed at AUCHEL. General preparation for inspection by the O.C. Brigade. No.844 @/Br. W.G.WATSON was transferred to Divisional Artillery Headquarters and was struck off the strength of the Brigade. 2 men from Base attached to Brigade Headquarters. 1 man returned from leave.	
	27th		A Brigade Inspection was carried out by the O.C. All Mess Carts, Water Carts and the Maltese Cart were inspected by the O.C. Divisional Train. Major POLLARD returned from leave. The Brigade Ammunition Column took 31 H.D. horses to LILLERS station and received in exchange 34 L.D. (Remounts) All men attached from Base were taken on the strength and posted to units.	
	28th		Lt. SPENCER and 12 men returned from leave. Lt. BOWDITCH joined the Brigade and was attached to Brigade Ammunition Column. A Church Parade was held in the morning and a route march (dismounted) was carried out in the afternoon. No.895 Gr. A.H.WILLCOX having rejoined the Brigade from Hospital was taken on the strength and	

Army Form C. 2118

WAR DIARY
or
INTELLIGENCE SUMMARY.

(Erase heading not required.)

Instructions regarding War Diaries and Intelligence Summaries are contained in F. S. Regs., Part II. and the Staff Manual respectively. Title pages will be prepared in manuscript.

Place	Date	Hour	Summary of Events and Information	Remarks and references to Appendices
FERFAY	28th		No.1138 Farrier Sergeant ANNETT was evacuated to ENGLAND and was posted to 22nd Battery. struck off strength.	
	29th		The Brigade Ammunition Column teamed their L.D. Remounts. 16 L.D.(remounts) exchanged with 16 L.D. from the Batteries. Preparations were made for a Divisional Route March to be carried out on 30th. Three days rations were drawn for Officers, N.C.Os. and men not proceeding on the Divisional Route March. At 7 p.m. a motor lorry arrived to carry horse rugs and spare blankets on the route march and the 2 drivers were attached for rations. The Route March was postponed for 24 hours. All Officers N.C.Os. and men returned from Courses. Lt. CAULFEILD STOKER and 7 men from Signal Co. and Lt. HENDERSON, 2/Lt. STEPHENSON, 2/Lt. LAWTHER and 8 N.C.Os. from Divisional Ammunition Colm. to take part in the Route March.	
	30th	7.15 a.m.	A party consisting of 2/Lt. STEPHENSON and 20 men were detailed for R.E. fatigues at CAUCHY A LA TOUR at 8.30 as per orders from Headquarters 47th Divisional Artillery. An agreement was entered into for use of pasture land at B.13.d.8.6. (Sheet 36b) for horse standings, and bricks were drawn and deposited there. In the Afternoon the preliminary orders for the route march were issued.	

Lt. Colonel R.F.A.(T.F.)

COMMANDING 8th LONDON (HOW.) F.A. BRIGADE.

Army Form C. 2118

WAR DIARY
or
INTELLIGENCE SUMMARY.

(Erase heading not required.)

Instructions regarding War Diaries and Intelligence Summaries are contained in F. S. Regs., Part II. and the Staff Manual respectively. Title pages will be prepared in manuscript.

Place	Date	Hour	Summary of Events and Information	Remarks and references to Appendices
LES BREBIS			**By MEDICAL OFFICER.** During November the health of the Brigade has been good, there being no cases of epidemic or contagious disease except two or of "scabies". There were some cases of "Chill" due to the inclement weather, but none of these were serious. No case of "Chilled Feet" has occurred in the Brigade.	
FERFAY			Since coming to FERFAY the system has been initated of having only one Incinerator and one refuse pit for the Brigade, these being under the care of permanent Sanitary Orderlies. The refuse from all units is brought to the Incinerator in sacks daily. This system has given better results than were obtained when each unit had a small separate Incinerator.	

J.F.Smith
Captain R.A.M.C.
Medical Officer,
i/c 8th London (How) F. A. Brigade.

1/8/81 (Inspn) Hon. Bae R.F.A.

Dei

v-r-X

Army Form C. 2118.

WAR DIARY
or
INTELLIGENCE SUMMARY.

(Erase heading not required.)

Instructions regarding War Diaries and Intelligence Summaries are contained in F. S. Regs., Part II. and the Staff Manual respectively. Title pages will be prepared in manuscript.

Place	Date	Hour	Summary of Events and Information	Remarks and references to Appendices
FERFAY B.18.b.2.3. Ref. Map 36.b. 1/40000	Decr. 1st.		**In Reserve.** The Brigade complete paraded in Field Service Marching Order at 8 am. and took part in a Divisional Route March. Route via ST.HILAIRE - ROMBLY arriving at ST.QUENTIN at 2.30 pm. Headquarters for the night were established at the CHATEAU, ST.QUENTIN. Batteries and B.A.C. in the village. Supplies arrived at 9 pm. Motor lorry with horse rugs did not arrive.	
	2nd.		Brigade received orders to return via AUCHY AU BOIS. Paraded at 8.50 am. and arrived at FERFAY 1.15 pm. On both out and return journey the Division was inspected by Lieut. General Sir H.RAWLINSON C.B.	
	3rd.		Brigade engaged on preparation of Horse Standings. Two Officers and 13 O.R.s proceeded on leave.	
	4th.		Brigade continued preparation of Horse Standings. Officers and N.C.O.s resumed their Course of Instruction at 47th Divisional Ammunition Column.	
	5th.	9.15 am.	Divine Service. G.O.C.R.A. attended and inspected the Brigade afterwards.	
	6th		Preparation of Standings continued. X Battery training carried out as far as possible. 3 men joined from Base. Lieut. F.P.Kindell returned from leave.	
	8th		Officers engaged on a tactical exercise. A. F.G.C.M. assembled for the purpose of trying 4 men of the 22nd Battery by F.G.C.M.	
	9th.		Preparation of Horse Standings continued, and 150 men obtained baths, at AUCHEL.	
	10th.		Preparation of Horse Standings continued and Battery training carried out. 28 O.Rs received and posted:- Headquarters - 1 21st Battery - 9. 22nd Battery - 10. and B.A.C. - 8. Tactical exercise for Officers with Battery Staffs. 2 Officers and 13 O.R.s granted leave.	
	11th.		Tactical exercise continued. Horse Standings carried on with. Promulgation of F.G.C.M. on 4 men of 22nd Battery. O.C. Brigade reconnoitred in locality of VERMELLES for new positions.	

Army Form C. 2118.

WAR DIARY
or
INTELLIGENCE SUMMARY.
(Erase heading not required.)

Instructions regarding War Diaries and Intelligence Summaries are contained in F. S. Regs., Part II. and the Staff Manual respectively. Title pages will be prepared in manuscript.

Place	Date	Hour	Summary of Events and Information	Remarks and references to Appendices
FERFAY.	Decr. 11th.		Lieut. Henderson returned from Course of Instruction at 47th Divisional Ammunition Column. Lieut. K.Webster and Lieut. A.L.Lawther and 13 O.R.s proceeded on leave.	
	12th.		Bathing Parade at AUCHEL. All Officers and men returned from Courses of Instruction. Sergt. Wellard, Ammunition Column granted one month's leave of absence on re-engagement. Lieut. S.Taylor and Lieut. W.H.Bevan and 15 O.R.s returned from leave.	
	13th.		Preparation of Horse Standing s continued. Battery Commanders left by motor lorry to reconnoitre positions.	
	14th.		Preparations made for the return to the Firing Line.	
	15th.		One Section of each Battery moved into action.	
NOYELLES K.K.a.K.X L.ll.d.3.0.	16th.		Remainder of Brigade moved up, and Lt.Col. E.H. ELEY assumed command of "ELEY GROUP consisting of the following:- Headquarters Position L.11.d.3.0. 21st Battery. A.25.c.3.3. 22nd Battery G.14.c.5.8. B.A.C. E.28d.9.5. Attached:- O 73rd Battery. G.14.c.4.6. 2nd Siege Battery G.13.b.5.7. (right section)	Ref. Map. 36 b. 1/40000 Trench Map. do Bethune combined sheet - 1/40000 Trench Map. do.
	17th.		Batteries in action, and registration carried out. From 2 p.m. to 3 p.m. the enemy bombarded our trenches in C.2 of our Divisional front with 77MM. from the direction of AUCHY and ST.ELIE.	
	18th.		Registration continued. Observation impossible owing to weather conditions. Enemy shelled various parts of our front with 4.2 H.E. and 77mm. Information received that we were to launch a gas attack along front R.I. North to the Canal about midnight. Wind unfavourable and attack postponed. Major ETON and 8 other ranks proceeded on leave.	

Army Form C. 2118.

WAR DIARY

~~INTELLIGENCE SUMMARY~~

(Erase heading not required.)

Instructions regarding War Diaries and Intelligence Summaries are contained in F.S. Regs., Part II. and the Staff Manual respectively. Title pages will be prepared in manuscript.

Place	Date	Hour	Summary of Events and Information	Remarks and references to Appendices
NOYELLES	Dec. 19th		Registration continued. Instructions received that 4th Corps Artillery and 47th Divisional Artillery will carry out a bombardment, with Heavy Howitzers and Field Guns, probably on the 20th at 11 a.m. Object to destroy suspected enemy mine shafts about G.4.b.5½.5, and G.4.b.2.4. One battery of ELEY GROUP to engage communication trenches running N.E. from "Cross Trench" to "Fosse Trench". (Reference Trench Map 36c.N.W.1 Prov: Edition No.2). Infantry to be withdrawn from our Front Line trenches. During registration a German was seen to be blown into the air. Wind very strong.	
	20th		Weather very misty - observation difficult. Retaliation carried out on various trenches opposite our front. Bombardment ordered on the 19th postponed. Gas attack ordered on 18th and postponed, to be launched at 10 p.m. Owing to a portion of ESSEX TRENCH having been captured this morning by enemy's bombers 47th Division Infantry twice attempted during the night to regain lost portion but failed. From 6.20 p.m. 20th to 2.15 a.m. 21st 22nd Battery bombarded trenches G.12.a.9.6. to G.12.a.4.6. and G.12.a.8½.7½. to G.6.c.1½.4. expending 210 rounds.	
	21st		Batteries continued registration. Weather very misty and bad for observation. O.C. 21st Battery assisted POOLE GROUP(9.2s) to register. 'Group' Commander attended conference of Group Commanders. Gas attack postponed from 18th inst. carried out. Zero time 8 p.m. Had no apparent effect on enemy. Vigorous shelling of our trenches by the enemy prevented any advantage being taken by us. We retaliated intermittently throughout the night. Lt. K. WEBSTER and 2/Lt. A.L. LAWTHER and 13 other ranks returned from leave.	
	22nd		Batteries engaged in further registration. Weather dull, misty and wet, not very suitable for observation of fire. A bombardment on the QUARRIES and CHORD was cancelled owing to Infantry not withdrawing from trenches. 22nd Battery assisted POOLE GROUP in registration. A similar gas attack to last night took place N. of LA BASSEE CANAL.	
	23rd		Weather fine and sunny during greater part of day. Germans shelled LE RUTOIRE and PHILOSOPHE with H.E. shells and shrapnel. Test concentration on QUARRIES took place at 2.40 p.m. At 3.30pm. a time test concentration on HOHENZOLLERN REDOUBT was made. Information received from 15th Division that horse left at FERFAY had been destroyed. Operation orders for 24th sent to each battery of Group.	
	24th		Weather showery but there were bright intervals with good light but much wind.	

Army Form C. 2118.

WAR DIARY

or

~~INTELLIGENCE SUMMARY.~~

(Erase heading not required.)

Instructions regarding War Diaries and Intelligence Summaries are contained in F. S. Regs., Part II. and the Staff Manual respectively. Title pages will be prepared in manuscript.

Place	Date	Hour	Summary of Events and Information	Remarks and references to Appendices

NOYELLES	Dec. 24th (contd)		At 7.18 a.m. 47th Division fired a mine at G.4.b.2.3. to 5.3. It was a success and was followed by considerable hostile artillery fire. Our operation fire ceased at 8.45 a.m. Batteries proceeded with registration. Experiments were made with Mark I and Mark II cartridges. Germans shelled VERMELLES with 5.9 Howitzers. LE RUTOIRE was again shelled. Time test concentration on "CHORD" took place at 3.50 p.m. Lt. Col. E.H.ELEY attended conference at Divisional Artillery, 47th Division. G.O.C.R.A. 47th Division sent Christmas Greetings to Artillery. Note: During bombardment that followed firing of mine The 2nd Siege Battery fired 33rounds
			                                      73rd "C" " 90
			                                      21st " " 117 "
			                                      22nd " " 120 "	

	25th		Weather wet with bright intervals and much wind. Batteries continued registration with exception of 2nd Siege Battery which did not fire during the day. Fosse 9 was shelled from direction of HAISNES at 1 p.m., Railway and Billets at ANNEQUIN at 6 p.m. by 77 mm. guns, Billets in PHILOSOPHE also shelled. We retaliated on HAISNES. Group Commander was informed that one section of 73rd "C" Battery would be relieved by 54th Division on night of 27th/28th instant. 2nd Siege Battery report first supply of A.P. shells. Orders received from Divisional Artillery to ease off expenditure of ammunition. Night fairly quiet and only 22nd Battery fired. Lt. E.R.COOPER and 8 other ranks granted leave to ENGLAND.	
	26th		Weather similar to yesterday. Group Commanders and Battery Commanders of 21st and 22nd Batteries made reconnaisance positions for howitzer group for VERMELLES, GRENAY, and SAILLY-LABOURSE Lines. very little firing done, 26 rounds only being fired by group. Lt. SPENCER reported for duty at Brigade headquarters.	
	27th		Weather gusty with sharp showers. Group Commander made further reconnaisances with O.C. 73rd "C" and 2nd Siege Batteries. Germans shelled ANNEQUIN and PHILOSOPHE frequently during day. Section of 73rd "C" Battery relieved by 2nd Suffolks during night. Fresh instructions for night firing received. Major ETON and 8 Other ranks returned from leave.	
	28th		Weather dry and fine. Batteries engaged most of day in Retaliation and Registration. Hostile aeroplane over 22nd and 73rd "C" Batteries' positions from 11 to 11.50 a.m. Instructions from 47th Divisional Artillery to fire on Trench Mortar in SLAG ALLEY. 73rd "C" Battery fired 36 rounds	

Army Form C. 2118.

WAR DIARY
or
INTELLIGENCE SUMMARY.

(Erase heading not required.)

Instructions regarding War Diaries and Intelligence Summaries are contained in F. S. Regs., Part II. and the Staff Manual respectively. Title pages will be prepared in manuscript.

Place	Date	Hour	Summary of Events and Information	Remarks and references to Appendices
NOYELLES	28th(contd)		on this trench and scored 17 hits in it. Group Commander attended conference at 47th Divisional Artillery in morning. Germans shelled following points during day:- Cross Roads in Philosophe, COROMS DE RUTOIRE and our trenches in D.1 and D.2 Sectors. G.11.b. & d with 4.2 and 5.9 H.E. and our trenches in G.5.c.c.	
	29th.		Weather fine and dry. G.O. attended conference at 47th Div. Arty. in morning. Hostile aeroplanes over 22nd Battery position in morning limited fire of that Battery. Enemy shelled front line and communication trenches in D.1 and D.2. Sectors most of the day. A bombardment of BILL'S BLUFF (G.5.a.6½.1), was made by 21st and C 73rd Batteries between 5pm and 5.30 pm. Each Battery fired 8 salvoes. Units informed that a supplementary Situation Report is to be sent in at 6.50 pm. daily for information of IVth Corps. Batteries continued registration during day.	
	30th.		Weather fine, sunny, but inclined to mist. Complaint from 21st Battery re bridges over trenches. R.E. taking necessary action. During day reports from Infantry that "HAIRPIN" heavily shelled. STIRLING GROUP and ELEY GROUP retaliated on QUARRIES, SLAG ALLEY, FOSSE ALLEY, GITE ST. ELIE. At 4.20 pm. enemy exploded mine near "HAIRPIN". Rifle fire, bombing and Artillery fire immediately developed on trenches affected. All Batteries of ELEY GROUP retaliated. Only 22nd Battery fired during night, (16 rounds into QUARRIES). 2/Lt. A.VICK reported from D.A.C. and attached to 21st Battery.	
	31st.		Weather dry and bright. Batteries continued registration. Hostile aeroplane over NOYELLES during morning. Group Headquarters heavily shelled with 4.2 H.E. shells from 12.30 pm to 2.50 pm (40 shells). Lieut. H.BOWDITCH detailed O.C. R.A.Dump at NOYELLES. Batteries warned concerning new positions, indents for material sent to D.A. 21st and 22nd Batteries only fired during night.	

Lt.Col. R.F.A. T.F.
Officer Commanding,
8th London (How) F.A. Brigade.

"A" Form.
MESSAGES AND SIGNALS.

Army Form C. 2121.

TO: Hqrs 47 D.A.

Sender's Number: E517
Day of Month: 6
AAA

Herewith recommendations as asked for ans A.7 W 3121 has been indented for but no supply received.

From: O.C. 8 Ton How
Time: 3p

8th LONDON (HOWITZER) BDE., R.F.A.,(T.F.), 47th LONDON DIVISION, IVth CORPS.

Schedule No.	Unit.	Regl. No.	Rank and Name.	Action for which commended.	Recommended by	Honour or Reward.
	22nd.Cty. of London Bty.,		Captain WALTER GEORGE LARGEN.	For several careful recon- naisances and reports on en- emy's positions and observa- tion stations and consistent good work during the past six months while in action. This Officer's good work during the battle of LOOS has previously been brought to notice.	Bde.Commander.	MENTION.
	21st.Cty. of London Bty.		2/Lieut.(Tempy Lieut) WILLIAM HUGH BEVAN	For consistent good work in observation of fire and handling of his battery while in action at VERMELLES and MAROC during the past three months.	Bde.Commander.	MENTION.

8th LONDON (HOWITZER) BDE., R.F.A.,(T.F.), 47th LONDON DIVISION, IVth CORPS.

Schedule No.	Unit.	Regl. No.	Rank and Name.	Action for which commended.	Recommended by	Honour or Reward.
	22nd C. of Lond Battery R.F.A.		Captain WALTER GEORGE LARGEN	For several careful reconnaissances and reports on enemy's positions and observation stations and consistent good work during the past six months while in action. This officer's good work during the battle of LOOS has previously been brought to notice.	Bde Commander	MENTION
	21st C. of Lond Battery R.F.A.		2nd Lieut (Temp/Lieut.) WILLIAM HUGH BEVAN	For consistent good work in observation of fire and handling of his battery whilst in action at VERMELLES and MAROC during the past three months	Bde Commander	MENTION

FILE 8

HISTORICAL SECTION
MILITARY BRANCH

1915 (Vol. I.)

YPRES, 1915

Sketch 13 _ Battle of St Julien, 25th April

(Corrected 1st Proof.)

Instructions enclosed

Index..........

SUBJECT.

HISTORICAL SECTION
MILITARY BRANCH.

FILE 2

No.	Contents.	Date.
	VOL II Additions to the black plates of Maps 6 and 7. (Instructions enclosed)	

47th Divisional Artillery

"238"

8 London (How) Bde

1916

8 London / Hon. R. A. Potter

Jan

Vol. X

Army Form C. 2118.

WAR DIARY

or

~~INTELLIGENCE SUMMARY.~~

(Erase heading not required.)

Instructions regarding War Diaries and Intelligence Summaries are contained in F.S. Regs., Part II. and the Staff Manual respectively. Title pages will be prepared in manuscript.

Place	Date	Hour	Summary of Events and Information	Remarks and references to Appendices
NOYELLES-Les-Vermelles	Jan. 1st		Weather stormy. Enemy shelled mine and billets ANNEQUIN. Batteries retaliated. Wind too strong for registration. Group Commander attended conference at 47th Divisional Artillery. 4 Remounts collected. 9 O.R.s proceeded on leave.	
	2nd		Weather fair. Enemy shelled communication trenches and neighbourhood of RUTOIRE, Railway and NOYELLES - CAMBRIN Road. Batteries engaged in retaliation most of day. Major E.ETON attached for Course of Instruction to M.G.R.A. Headquarters.	
	3rd		Weather fine. Group Headquarters shelled with 4.2" H.E. from 8.30 am. to 10 am. Building hit in several places. About 60 shells (Shrapnel and H.E.) were fired at the farm. No casualties. Horses safely removed under fire. Group Headquarters moved to L.10.b.6.3. ref. map 36.B N.E. 1/20,000. 8 O.R.s returned from leave.	
L.10.b.6.3.	4th.		Weather stormy. Moderate enemy shelling. Batteries retaliated. Lieut. E.R.COOPER returned from leave.	
	5th.		Orders received Division to be relieved by Dismounted Division. This Group by 4th London (How) Bde. R.F.A. A bombardment of the MOUND in QUARRIES, CORONS West of DUMP, Cité St.ELIE and trenches carried out. Brigade Ammunition Column moved to HOUCHIN.	
	6th.		Weather stormy. Retaliation carried out. One Section each of 21st and 22nd Batteries, moved into new positions.	
	7th.		Weather stormy. Remaining sections of Brigade, 2nd Siege Battery, and Group Headquarters moved into their new positions as follows:- Group Headquarters L.35.d.9.9. Ref. Map 36.b. N.E. 1/20,000. 21st Battery. M.2.d.2.2.) 22nd Battery M.2.d.4.4.) " " 36 C N.W. 1/20,000 Edition 6. C 73rd Btty. M.2.d.2.5.) 2nd Siege Battery G.32.d.6.2)	

Army Form C. 2118.

WAR DIARY
or
INTELLIGENCE SUMMARY.
(Erase heading not required.)

Instructions regarding War Diaries and Intelligence Summaries are contained in F.S. Regs., Part II. and the Staff Manual respectively. Title pages will be prepared in manuscript.

Place	Date	Hour	Summary of Events and Information	Remarks and references to Appendices
GRENAY L.35.d.9.9.	Jan. 8th		Major E.ETON returned from attachment to M.G.R.A. Headquarters. Batteries carried out registration. Lieut. T.CAULFEILD STOKER and 2Lt. R.W.MILES and 7 O.R.s granted 7 days leave of absence.	
	9th		Registration continued. 21st Battery Carried out a bombardment of a portion of enemy front line trench. 9 O.R.s returned from leave.	
	10th		Batteries registering and retaliating. Battery Wagon lines moved from LES BREBIS to NOEUX LES MINES. 30 O.R.s attached to 47th Divisional Ammunition Column. C.R.A. and Group Commander for x reconnoitred for new positions for a section of 2nd Siege Battery R.G.A. Position chosen L.36.c.5.3½.	
	12th to 14th		Registration and retaliation carried out. Enemy's artillery active on LOOS and MAROC.	
	15th		Lt.Col.E.H.ELMY granted 10 days leave of absence. Major E.ETON assumed the duties of Group Commander. Lieut. J.W.HENDERSON and 2/Lt.G.A.E. STEPHENSON and 7 O.R.s granted 7 days leave.	
	16th to 18th.		Retaliation and intermittent shelling of enemy's transport centres and traffic routes.	
	19th		4.5" Howitzer equipment to replace 5" Equipment taken over at BETHUNE STATION. Guns overhauled and made ready at the wagon lines. 4.5" ammunition drawn from 47th Divisional Ammunition Column.	
	20th		About 7 pm. a section of 4.5" Hows. replaced a section of 5" Hows. in each Battery. 4 O.R.s received from 47th D.A.C.	
	21st		Registration with the 4.5" Hows. carried out. Remaining sections of 5"Hows. withdrawn and 4.5" Hows. substituted.	

Army Form C. 2118.

WAR DIARY
or
INTELLIGENCE SUMMARY.
(Erase heading not required.)

Instructions regarding War Diaries and Intelligence Summaries are contained in F. S. Regs., Part II. and the Staff Manual respectively. Title pages will be prepared in manuscript.

Place	Date	Hour	Summary of Events and Information	Remarks and references to Appendices
L.35.d.9.9.	Jan. 22nd		Registration continued. Capt. J.F.SMITH R.A.M.C., Capt. W.G.LARGEN and 15 O.R.s granted 7 days leave.	
	23rd		At 2 a.m. a British mine was fired at M.6.a.1½.1. and 21st Battery formed a barrage on the enemy trenches opposite in M.6.a. and c. The crater was successfully occupied by our Infantry and named HARRISON'S CRATER. 5" Equipment entrained at BETHUNE for ENGLAND. Hostile aeroplanes overhead prevented much firing during the day.	
	24th		Registration continued. Lieut. J.W.HENDERSON, 2/LIEUT G.A.E.STEPHENSON and 7 O.R.s returned from leave.	
	25th		Hostile aircraft unusually active, and prevented registration. Enemy's artillery carried out concentrated fire on various portions of our trenches. During the day 10 trains were observed passing the METALLURGIQUE in a Southerly direction.	
	26th		Observation difficult. Our front line and support trenches heavily shelled with H.E. and Shrapnel throughout the day. Lt. Col. E.H.ELEY returned from leave.	
	27th		Registration continued. Howitzer No.746 of 21st Battery damaged through a premature. - Fuze No.100 used - Howitzer sent to Ordnance Workshop and condemned. New one indented for. Heavy shelling of whole area by hostile artillery.	5" L.522
	28th		Enemy continued his bombardment of our front line and communication trenches, - specially heavy near the COPSE and LOOS CRASSIER. Gas and lachrymatory shells were used freely by the enemy and fired into MAROC and GRENAY.	
	29th		General hostile shelling continued. Group retaliated. At 6.50 pm. another premature occurred in the 21st Battery when using No.100 fuze. Premature occurred about 50 yards from the gun without inflicting any casualties.	

Army Form C. 2118.

WAR DIARY
or
INTELLIGENCE SUMMARY.
(Erase heading not required.)

Instructions regarding War Diaries and Intelligence
Summaries are contained in F. S. Regs., Part II.
and the Staff Manual respectively. Title pages
will be prepared in manuscript.

Place	Date	Hour	Summary of Events and Information	Remarks and references to Appendices
L.35.d.9.9.	Jan. 30th		Heavy mist all day. Only aggressive rounds were fired on enemy's transport and billeting centre in CITE St.LAURENT. 4 L.D. and 6 Riders received.	
	31st		Observation difficult. Retaliation carried out.	

Lt. Col. R.F.A. T.F.
Officer Commanding,
8th London (How) F.A. Brigade.

47

1/8 London Bde R.F.A
Feb
Vol XIX

Army Form C. 2118.

WAR DIARY
or
INTELLIGENCE SUMMARY.
(Erase heading not required.)

Instructions regarding War Diaries and Intelligence Summaries are contained in F.S. Regs., Part II. and the Staff Manual respectively. Title pages will be prepared in manuscript.

Place	Date	Hour	Summary of Events and Information	Remarks and references to Appendices
GRENAY L.35.d.9.9	Feb. 1st.		Registration carried out. Batteries fired on suspected enemy transport routes and billets. Premature with a No.100 Fuze No.2 Gaine in the 21st Battery. No damage to material or personnel. Weather fine. 2 Riders and 3 L.D.s received.	
	2nd.		Registration and aggressiveness continued. Lieut. Harding relieved from attachment at D.A.C. by Lieut. Stephenson.	
	3rd.		Aggressiveness carried out. Several important enemy earthworks bombarded with good effect. Weather fine. Strong Easterly wind. Reported enemy mine fired at 5 p.m. Barrages established immediately. Report proved false. 30 O.R's returned from Attachment to D.A.C.	
	4th.		Registration. 1 O.R. evacuated. 1 O.R. transferred from D.A.C. B.176 Battery R.F.A. and section of Ammn. Col. joined the Brigade on augmentation of Establishment. Strength:- Battery – 4 Officers, 25 N.C.O's, 102 Men, 4 A.V.C Sergeant, 2 A.S.C O.R's, 1 Gunner for watercart duties. 125 horses, 4 A.S.C horses, 14 four-wheeled vehicles, 2 two-wheeled vehicles, 108 rounds of ammunition; Ammn. Column– 25 N.C.O's and Men, 33 L.D's, 2 H. D's, 4 limbered wagons, 1 G.S wagon.	
	5th.		Registration and aggressiveness carried out. 1N Section of 176 Battery relieved a Section of 30/A Battery at 7 p.m. 1N officer and 15 O.R's proceeded on leave.	
	6th.		Registration and aggressiveness. Lieut. Col. Eley attached to M.G.R.A. Headquarters, AIRE. for a Course of Instruction. Major Eton assumed command of Group. Remaining Section of B. 175 Battery moved into position and relieved Section of 30/A Battery. 1 Officer and 7 O.R's proceeded on leave.	
	7th.		Registration and aggressiveness. 1N Corporal and 5 Men attached to batteries from 4th. Corps Ammn. Park and a like number attached from batteries to 4th. Corps Park. 11 O.R's returned from leave.	
	8th.		Group Commander interviewed Lieut. Col. Massey C.R.A., 47th. Division, as to formation of advanced wagon lines for the batteries of the Eley Group, and was informed the lines could not be authorised. Arrangements were made with Lt. Col. Peal for the Eley Group to have the useof the Peal Group wire to the wagon line at the Corons de Braquemont. Aggressiveness. 3 O.R's returned from leave.	
	9th. & 10th.		Aggressiveness.	
	11th.		Lieut. Col. Eley returned from attachment at M.G.R.A. Field Officers' Course.	
	12th.		Aggressiveness. Enemy exploded a mine at M.6.c.4.5. at 6.45.a.m. Few Casualties, but attempt to occupy crater was met by our M.G fire and repulsed. Eley Group formed a pre-arranged barrage.	
	13th.			
	14th.		Aggressiveness. 1 Officer and 16 O.R's returned from leave.	
	15th.		Aggressiveness. Operation Orders received. Brigade to move with Division into G.H.Q Reserve, ready to entrain at 9 hrs. notice. 2 Officers & 14 Men proceeded on leave	

Army Form C. 2118.

WAR DIARY
or
INTELLIGENCE SUMMARY.
(Erase heading not required.)

Instructions regarding War Diaries and Intelligence Summaries are contained in F. S. Regs., Part II. and the Staff Manual respectively. Title pages will be prepared in manuscript.

Place	Date	Hour	Summary of Events and Information	Remarks and references to Appendices
L.35.d.9.9.	16th.		21st. Battery remains in action as a Counter- Battery and placed under orders of Poole Group. "B" Section of the 22nd. and B/176 Battery relieved by the 1st. D.A. 1 O.R returned from leave.	
	17th.		Night relieved a mine at 7 a.m. near Harts Crater. Remaining relief sections of 1st. D.A. took over from 22nd. and B/176 Batteries.	
Ferfay.	18th.		Brigade moved to FERFAY. 2 O.R's proceeded on leave.	
	19th.		1 W.O.R's taken on Brigade strength from Base, via D.A.C. Brigade marched to AUCHEL for baths.	
Erny St. Julien.	20th.		Brigade (less 21st. Battery) moved to ERNY ST. JULIEN. 5 O.R's reported for Course at 4th. Corps Signals.	
	21st.		Training in Gun drill, Laying, Signalling, Range finding, Musketry and foot drill. 2 officers and 9 O.R's returned from leave. 2 officers and 6 Men proceeded on leave.	
Reclinghem and Dennebroeucq.	22nd.		Brigade moved to new training area at REGLINGHEM and DENNEBROEUCQ	
	23rd.		Training continued.	
	24th.		Captain Cowan reported to 1st. Army School for Trench Mortar Course. Training continued.	
	25th.		Training continued. 2 officers and 7 Men proceeded on leave.	
	26th.		Inspection by G.O. of harness and equipment. Received from D.A. Operation Order as to relief of 21st. Battery in action by 22nd. Battery, on 3rd/4th. March.	
	27th.		Officers' Staff Ride in which Battery Staffs and Signallers took part.	
	28th.		Training continued. O's C. units arranged schemes and exercised their staffs around ERNY ST. JULIEN. 6 O.R's taken on strength from Base via D.A.C. Captn. Cowan returned from Course.	
	29th.		Training continued. 1 Rider and N.L.D's collected from D.A.C. Operation Order received on the 26th. cancelled.	

S.K Cosper Lt. Colo.
for Lieut. Colonel, R.F.A., T.F.,
Officer Commanding,
8th. London (How) B.A. Brigade.

2353 Wt. W25ll/1454 700,000 5/15 D.D.&L. A.D.S.S./Forms/C. 2118.

47

1/8 London Bde
R.F.A.

Vol XIII

Army Form C. 2118.

WAR DIARY
or
INTELLIGENCE SUMMARY.
(Erase heading not required.)

Instructions regarding War Diaries and Intelligence Summaries are contained in F.S. Regs., Part II. and the Staff Manual respectively. Title pages will be prepared in manuscript.

Place	Date	Hour	Summary of Events and Information	Remarks and references to Appendices
Reclinghem and Dennebroeucq	Mar. 1st		The Brigade (less 21st Battery, in action) continued training.	
	2nd		Training continued. 6 O.R.s arrived from Base, taken on strength, and posted to B/176 Battery.	
	3rd		Training continued. 3 O.R.s proceeded to Cadet School, England with a view to taking up Commissions.	
	4th		Training continued.	
	5th 6th		Training continued. Rev. A.E.Wilkinson, C.F., attached to Brigade.	
	7th		Training continued. Practice close attack at night on billeting area. 22nd Battery moved to AUCHEL to relieve 21st Battery at MAROC.	
	8th to 11th		Training continued. 21st Bty. relieved by 22nd Bty. moved to CALONNE RICOUART.	
Calonne Ricouart and Fosse de Clarence	12th		Brigade (less 21st and 22nd Batteries moved to:- Hdqtrs. - CALONNE RICOUART 21st Bty. ditto. B/176 & Ammunition Column; FOSSE DE CLARENCE.	
	13th		Training continued.	
	14th		Training continued. G.O. inspected 21st Battery. G.O.C., R.A., inspected an Officers' Ride.	
	15th		Training continued. C.O. and Battery Commanders reconnoitred new battery positions. Major E. ETON left for England.	
	16th		Training continued.	
	17th		One section of 21st and B/176 Batteries moved into action on new Divisional Front relieving 25rd Divisional Artillery in the CARENCY Section.	

Army Form C. 2118.

WAR DIARY
or
INTELLIGENCE SUMMARY.
(Erase heading not required.)

Instructions regarding War Diaries and Intelligence Summaries are contained in F. S. Regs., Part II. and the Staff Manual respectively. Title pages will be prepared in manuscript.

Place	Date	Hour	Summary of Events and Information	Remarks and references to Appendices
Calonne Ricouart and Fosse de Clarence	17th (contd)		21st Batty. attached to Northern Group (7th Lon. F.A.B.-Lt.-Col. PEALE	
	22nd		" " " Southern " (5th Lon. F.A.B.- " Massy)	
			B/176 " " " Centre " (6th Lon. F.A.B.- " Lowe)	
			Guns of 23rd Div. Arty. were left in position and guns of 47th Div. Arty. exchanged.	
	19th		Remaining sections and B.A.C. moved into action.	
	20th		Brigade Headquarters moved to FREVILLERS. Battery wagon lines and B.A.C. established at CAUCOURT. Area taken over in filthy condition.	
	22nd		Capt. A.J.Gowan posted to command 21st Battery vice Major E. Eton to England. Lt. Kindell to 1st Army School of Instruction at LIETTRES.	
	23rd		12 O.R.s of 47th D.A.C. interchanged with 12 O.R.s of the Batteries for instruction (4 attached to each battery). 6 L.D. horses received and posted to B/176 Battery.	
	25th		17 O.R.s arrived from the Base and are taken on the strength. Capt.Clarke,47th D.A.C. attd. to 21st Batty.	
	26th		Lieut. E.R.Cooper, Lieut. W.H.Bevan and 10 O.R.s proceeded on leave.	
	27th		Capt.Clarke returned to D.A.C. Capt.White,47th D.A.C. attd. 21st Battery.	
	28th		5 O.R.s on arrival from the Base, were taken on the strength.	
	~~29th~~ 30th		Capt. White returned to D.A.C.	
			12 O.R.s attached to Batteries returned to 47th D.A.C. 12 O.R.s attached 47th D.A.C. returned to Batteries.	

E.J.Rey
Lt.-Col., R.F.A., T.F.,
Commanding,
8th London (now) F. A. Brigade.

COPY.

Secret.

M.G., R.A., 1st. Army No. O/39/2.

G.O.C., R.A., IVth. Corps.

The recent German offensive at VERDUN brought out certain points in the organisation of the French Artillery to resist an attack in force, and the G.O.C., 1st. Army, wishes me to bring them to your notice.

1. In some cases the Observation posts were not given a sufficient field of view, or as much as could have been given, with the result that the german attack in many places was soon out of sight, and sufficient artillery fire could not be brought to bear on the attack.

2. When the O.P's in the front line trenches were rushed, there were no alternative positions in rear which could be occupied, and consequently fire could not be brought on the front line trenches to shell the Germans out of them.

Will you please let me know that these points have received full consideration in the selection and construction of O.P's on your Corps Front. As regards 2, it is of course essential that alternative O.P's on the telephone line to a forward O.P., should be selected, so that the O.O. can at once move back to one and be in communication with his battery.

Would you also, at your convenience, let me have a list of all the O.P's., by map co-ordinates, on your Front.

H.Q., 1st. Army. (sd) F.Mercer,
6th.March,1916. M.G., R.A.

****

To O.C:- 21st. Battery.
        22nd. Battery.
        176/B Battery.
        Ammn. Column.
        Orderly Officer.
....

Forwarded for your information.

Lieut. R.F.A., T.F.,
Adjutant,

ES/632.

16/3/16. 8th. London (How) F.A. Brigade.

Army Form C. 2118.

WAR DIARY
or
INTELLIGENCE SUMMARY.
(Erase heading not required.)

Instructions regarding War Diaries and Intelligence Summaries are contained in F.S. Regs., Part II. and the Staff Manual respectively. Title pages will be prepared in manuscript.

Place	Date	Hour	Summary of Events and Information	Remarks and references to Appendices
FREVILLERS	April 1st 2nd 3rd		Lieut.-Col. E. H. Eley assumed command of the LEFT GROUP of the 47th Divisional Artillery. The D.D.V.S. and D.D.R. inspected the horses of the Brigade at GAUCOURT. 1 Officer and 14 O.R.s proceeded on leave.	
	4th		Lecture to Officers by Corps Commander. Wagon Line of "R"/8th Battery moved from GAUCOURT to X.13.b and d. (in the wood), reference map Sheet 36b., 1/40000. One Officer and 9 O.R.s returned from leave. 1 O.R. proceeded on leave.	
	5th		8 Telephonists of Brigade Headquarters attached to LEFT GROUP for duty.	
	8th		Lieut. Kindell returned from a course at 1st Army Artillery School, LIETTRES.	
	9th		13 O.R.s on arrival from the Base were taken on the strength of the Brigade and attached to the Batteries. 1 O.R. proceeded on one month's leave on re-engagement.	
	10th		2/Lieut. E. A. de Burgh West attached to the B.A.C.	
	11th		2 Officers and 14 O.R.s proceeded on 7 days leave and 2 Officers returned from leave.	
	13th		8th London (How) F.A.B. Headquarters took over the LEFT GROUP from the 7th London F.A.B. Hd. Qrs. Course of Instruction for Corporals was commenced at the Wagon Line GAUCOURT.	
	14th		Mine exploded by us at 3 a.m.	
	15th		Enemy artillery fairly active.	
	16th		Capt. A.J.Cowan promoted Major vice "Eton" to England and Lieut. F.P.Kindell, Captain vice "Cowan".	
	17th		Lecture by Corps Commander to remainder of Officers of the Division (previous lecture on the 4th).	
	18th		Brigade Headquarters relieved Headquarters of the 8th London F.A.B. at the RIGHT GROUP Hd.Qrs.	

Army Form C. 2118.

WAR DIARY
or
INTELLIGENCE SUMMARY.
(Erase heading not required.)

Instructions regarding War Diaries and Intelligence Summaries are contained in F. S. Regs., Part II. and the Staff Manual respectively. Title pages will be prepared in manuscript.

Place	Date	Hour	Summary of Events and Information	Remarks and references to Appendices
	April 19th		1 Rider and 6 Light Draught (remounts) collected and also 5 Light Draughts for Draught for R/8th Btty.	
	21st		R/8th Btty. had 1 man killed. 4 O.R.s on arrival from the Base were taken on the strength of the Brigade.	
	25th		Mine exploded and crater occupied by enemy on 46th Division Front. Batteries formed a barrage. Captain Largen, 22nd Battery, transferred to command Brigade Ammunition Column.	
	26th		Lt.-Col. E. H. Eley proceeded on 10 days leave. Another mine was exploded by the enemy on the 46th Division Front. Enemy artillery active.	
	28th		2 Officers and 19 O.R.s proceeded on leave. Brigade Headquarters relieved by the 5th Brigade Hd. Qrs.	
	30th		3 Officers and 3 N.C.O.s left to attend an Artillery Course at MAGNICOURT, 1 O.R. to attend a Signalling Course at PERNES and 1 O.R. to attend a Course on Trench Warfare at PERNES.	

[signature]
Major, R.F.A.,T.F.,
Commanding,
8th London (How) F.A. Brigade.

P.S.:- The Batteries of this Brigade were attached during the month and grouped for tactical purposes with the 5th, 6th and 7th London Field Artillery Brigades.

"A" Form.
MESSAGES AND SIGNALS.
Army Form C. 2121.

Secret

TO: D.A.G., 3rd Echelon

Sender's Number	Day of Month	In reply to Number	
E171	3rd		AAA

Herewith War Diary for Brigade for month of May

From O.C., 238th Brigade, R.F.A.

238 Bde RZ
Me /8 London Bde
Vol 15

Army Form C. 2118.

WAR DIARY
or
INTELLIGENCE SUMMARY.
(Erase heading not required.)

Instructions regarding War Diaries and Intelligence Summaries are contained in F. S. Regs., Part II. and the Staff Manual respectively. Title pages will be prepared in manuscript.

Place	Date	Hour	Summary of Events and Information	Remarks and references to Appendices
FREVILLERS.	May, 1916. 1st.		Brigade Headquarters at rest. 21st and R/8 Battery in action attached to Left Group, 47th Div.Arty. 22nd Battery in action and attached to Right Group, 47th Div. Arty.	
	3rd.		Capt.W.E.Taylor, 2/8th London (How) F. A. Brigade reported for 2 weeks attachment to 21st Battery.	
	5th.		2 Off. and 19 O.R.s proceeded on leave.	
	6th.		Headquarters relieved Headquarters of Right Group, 47th Div. Arty. at X.7.c.5.5. Ref. Map 36b. This Group was comprised of 15th, 16th, and 17th London Batteries, R/6 Battery, (1/40,000) 22nd London Battery, and R/8 Battery.	
	7th.		Lt.Col.E.H.Eley and 2/Lieut.R.W.Miles returned from leave. Lt.Col.Eley assumed command of Right Group. Capt.A.McKinnon, R.A.M.C., attached for duty.	
	8th.		Enemy fired a mine on 25th Division Front; no attack followed.	
	9th.		16th London Battery and R/8 Battery positions were heavily shelled with 5.9's. About 130 rounds fell in and about the positions but there were no casualties. At 7.30 p.m. the enemy fired 2 mines, one on 47th Division Front and another on 25th Division Front. Barrage opened and maintained for 1 hour.	
	10th.		Intermittent shelling on both sides.	
	11th.		Capt. W. Largen, B.A.C., transferred to England.	
	12th.		Major. C. Bollard and 13 O.R.s proceeded on leave. Capt. F. De Witt, posted from 21st Battery to command BAC. Capt. H. McVeagh, supernumerary, absorbed and posted to 21st Battery.	
	13th.		2 Off. and 19 O.R.s returned from leave. Quiet day on the Front.	

Army Form C. 2118.

WAR DIARY
or
INTELLIGENCE SUMMARY.
(Erase heading not required.)

Instructions regarding War Diaries and Intelligence Summaries are contained in F.S. Regs., Part II. and the Staff Manual respectively. Title pages will be prepared in manuscript.

Place	Date	Hour	Summary of Events and Information	Remarks and references to Appendices
X.7.c.5.5.	14th.		Orders were received to adopt new nomenclature as follows :- 8th London (How) F.A. Brigade Headquarters to form Headquarters of 238th Brigade, R.F.A. 21st London Battery renamed D/238th Battery and posted to 238th Brigade. 22nd London Battery renamed D/236th Battery and posted to 236th Brigade. R/8 Battery renamed D/235th Battery and posted to 235th Brigade. B.A.C. absorbed in the 47th D.A.C. 238th Brigade to comprise :- Headquarters, 8th London (HOW) F.A. Brigade. 34th Battery, R.F.A. B/238th Battery, R.F.A. C/238th Battery, R.F.A. D/238th Battery, R.F.A. 2/Lieut. G. Stephenson, Supernumerary, absorbed and posted to D/238th Battery. 2/Lieut. A. Lawther, Supernumerary, absorbed and posted to D/235th Battery. Lieut. J. Henderson, B.A.C., posted to D/235th Battery. Capt. McKinnon, R.A.M.C., ceased attachment to Right Group.	Authority:- O.B./818, 1st Army, G.S.290.
	17th/18th & 19th.		Enemy's Minenwerfers very active on our communication trenches. Retaliation carried out by Heavy Artillery and Field Batteries.	
	19th		15 O.R.'s proceeded on leave.	
FREVILLERS.	20th		Lieut.-Col. Peal, 237th Brigade, relieved Headquarters 238th Brigade; Headquarters returned to rest at FREVILLERS.	
	21st		At 10p.m. orders were received to proceed with Headquarters and assist Left Group, 47th Div Arty.; Enemy attacked on our front and gained possession of a portion of our trenches on the VIMY RIDGE.	

T134. Wt. W708—776. 500000. 4/15. Sir J.C. & S.

Army Form C. 2118.

WAR DIARY
or
INTELLIGENCE SUMMARY.
(Erase heading not required.)

Instructions regarding War Diaries and Intelligence Summaries are contained in F. S. Regs., Part II. and the Staff Manual respectively. Title pages will be prepared in manuscript.

Place	Date	Hour	Summary of Events and Information	Remarks and references to Appendices
FREVILLERS.	May 22nd.	2 a.m.	Lt.Col.Eley and Signallers remained with Left Group. Remainder of Headquarters returned to FREVILLERS.	
	23rd.		Lieut. & Adjutant E. R. Cooper attached to 141st Infantry Brigade, at advance Headquarters, as Liaison Officer. British counter-attacked to recover trenches lost on VIMY RIDGE on 21st instant. Artillery cooperated.	
	26th.		Lt.Col.Eley returned from attachment to Left Group. Lieut. E. R. Cooper returned from attachment to 141st Infantry Brigade. B/238th and D/238th moved out of action to DIVION.	
DIVION.	27th.		Headquarters removed to DIVION. C/238th moved out of action to DIVION.	
	28th.		Brigade under 4 hours notice whilst with Division in reserve.	
	29th.		Orders to move from DIVION to BARLIN and arrive at BARLIN at 1 p.m.	
BARLIN.	31st.		C/238th Battery went into action and attached to 1st Corps for Tactics and Administration.	

S.M. Eley

Lt.Col., R.F.A., T.F.,
Commanding,
238th Brigade, R.F.A.

47

234 Bde RFA

Vol 16

WAR DIARY
or
INTELLIGENCE SUMMARY.

Army Form C. 2118.

(Erase heading not required.)

Place	Date	Hour	Summary of Events and Information	Remarks and references to Appendices
BARLIN	1st June		The Brigade, less 34th and D/238th Batteries, in reserve.	
	2nd		15 O.Rs. (reinforcements) and 2 Light Draught horses from D.A.C. posted to 'B' and 'D' Batteries 2 Officers (Major Cowan and Capt. Cotter) and 13 O.Rs. proceeded on leave.	
	3rd		Capt. H. Jacoby, 3/2nd London Brigade R.F.A. reported and was attached to D/238th Battery.	
	5th		Maj.-Gen. Sir C. St. L. Barter, K.C.B., Commanding 47th (London) Division, inspected Head-quarters and Batteries of Brigade in BARLIN. 1 O.R. proceeded on leave.	
	9th		2 Officers (2/Lt. M.Williams and 2/Lt. J.S.Innes) and 10 O.Rs. proceeded on leave.	
	10th		13 O.Rs. returned from leave. 1 O.R. proceeded on 1 month's leave on re-engagement.	
	11th		Church Parade on D/238th Battery Wagon Park.	
	14th		Lt.-Col. E.H.Eley reconnoitred positions for guns for Camouflage operations. Working party commenced work on positions and continued daily.	
	14th-16th		Batteries of Brigade moved into action as follows :- C/238th and D/238th Batteries to Left Group (Lt.-Col. E.C.Massey). 34th and B/238th Batteries to Counter Battery work.	
BOYEFFLES	16th		Brigade Headquarters moved from BARLIN to BOYEFFLES Chateau. Lieutenant and Adjutant E.R. Cooper temporarily attached for duty to Left Group. Work continued on Camouflage positions which were const ructed at the following points :- M.34.a.: R.17.a. 4.5.: R.17.c.0.8.: R.33.b.: R.27.c. and R.27.a. A single gun and howitzer were placed at the disposal of Lt.-Col. E.H.Eley, C.M.G. for Camouflage registration. Os.C. Batteries, in turn, daily registered points commencing from the 16th June. The opera-tions carried out by each Battery Commander were as follows :- Six rounds were fired at intervals during the night and three or four points were registered on enemy's trench system in ANGRES Sector during the day. Each Battery used 36 rounds of ammunition to carry out this work. Similar operations were carried out and systematic registration made with a	

Army Form C. 2118.

WAR DIARY
or
INTELLIGENCE SUMMARY.
(Erase heading not required.)

Instructions regarding War Diaries and Intelligence Summaries are contained in F. S. Regs., Part II. and the Staff Manual respectively. Title pages will be prepared in manuscript.

Place	Date	Hour	Summary of Events and Information	Remarks and references to Appendices
BOYEFFLES	16th June.		4.5 inch howitzer. At times during the construction of the positions and after occupation hostile shelling took place with L.H.V. and 4.2 inch. Operations ceased on the 25th June.	
	17th		2 Officers and 10 O.Rs. returned from leave.	
	20th		Lt. and Adjutant E.R. Cooper ceased attachment to Left Group.	
	21st		2 Light Draught horses collected from D.A.C. Captain R.K.Cotter returned from leave. 1 O.R. proceed on leave.	
	22nd		2/Lieut. I.A. Masson, B/238th Battery attached to a Trench Mortar Battery. 2/Lieut. W.B. Foord-Kelcey posted to Brigade and attached to B/238th Battery.	
	24th		1 O.R. proceeded on leave.	
	25th		No. 48314, Sergt. Jackson joined 2M C/238th Battery from D/280th Battery R.F.A.	
	27th		Lt.-Col. E.H.Eley, C.M.G. attached to 141st Infantry Brigade to represent 47th Divisional Artillery during the operations carried out on the night of the 27th/28th.	

Eley
Lt.-Col.,R.F.A., T.F.,
Commanding,
238th Brigade R.F.A.

47th Divisional Artillery.

238th BRIGADE

ROYAL FIELD ARTILLERY.

JULY 1916

WAR DIARY
or
INTELLIGENCE SUMMARY.
(Erase heading not required.)

Army Form C. 2118.

235th Brigade R.F.A.

Vol 17

Place	Date	Hour	Summary of Events and Information	Remarks and references to Appendices
	July			
BOYEFFLES	1st-9th		Brigade Headquarters resting at BOYEFFLES. Batteries in action as follows:- 34th Bty ⎫ attached to 14th Corps Heavy Group B/238th ⎬ for Counter Battery work (Lt.Col. E.C. MASSY) C/238th ⎫ attached to Left Group for Tactical D/238th ⎬ work	
	5th		Lieut. and Adjutant E.R. Cooper attached to 47th Divl. Arty. on Staff duties.	
	7th		Lt. J.I. Beever, 47th D.A.C. attached to Brigade Headquarters for duty.	
	9th		2/Lt. B.J. DANIEL and 2/Lt. B. HENSHALL, both from England attached to Brigade for duty.	
	10th		Lt. Col. E.H. ELEY, Q.M.G, and 238th Brigade Headquarters relieved Lt. Col. E.C. MASSY and 235th Brigade Headquarters at Left Group. The group consisted of the following batteries:- A/235, C/235, C/238, D/238, A/223, and	

WAR DIARY
or
INTELLIGENCE SUMMARY.
(Erase heading not required.)

Army Form C. 2118.

Instructions regarding War Diaries and Intelligence Summaries are contained in F. S. Regs., Part II. and the Staff Manual respectively. Title pages will be prepared in manuscript.

Place	Date	Hour	Summary of Events and Information	Remarks and references to Appendices
			X/147th and Z/147th Trench Mortar Batteries. A, B and C Btys 318th Bde, (Royal Naval Division) reported - 9 officers and 84 O.Rs, and were attached to A, B and C Btys, 235th Bde, respectively. B.G,R.A. issued instructions for A & C/235th to reconnoitre positions for forward gun to shoot BULLY CRATER.	
		11th	Instructions issued for batteries to register enemy 2nd line, S.I. to M.36 (Ref. Map. 36c. S.W. 1/20,000) and a How. Battery to register SOUCHEZ RIVER, M.28 d. and eastwards.	
		12th 13th 14th	Work commenced on emplacements for T.M. B.tys. Wire cutting by T.M. B.tys. with covering fire from A and B/235th Bde. Gaps were made in enemy's wire. Major H.S.6. Crozier M.G. Corps took over machine gun duties.	
		15th	318th Bde. personnel attached for instruction were transferred to Right Group, 315th and 317th Bdes (R.N.D.) personnel attached to LEFT GROUP for instruction with a view to taking over. Wire cutting continued by T.M. B.tys.	

Army Form C. 2118.

WAR DIARY
or
INTELLIGENCE SUMMARY.
(Erase heading not required.)

Instructions regarding War Diaries and Intelligence Summaries are contained in F. S. Regs., Part II. and the Staff Manual respectively. Title pages will be prepared in manuscript.

Place	Date	Hour	Summary of Events and Information	Remarks and references to Appendices
	16th		Wire cutting continued by T.M. Btys. Covering fire by Bande C.235 Bde.	
	17th	11am-11.30am	47th Div Arty. Op. Order duly carried out. B/235, C/235, C/238 and D/238 forming a barrage across Salient in M.26.C. (Ref Map 31. t.S.W.1)	
	19th		Arrangements made and sanction for forward enfilading guns :- (1) C/238 at M.14.C.1.3.; (2) D/238 (-How.) at M.14.C.4½.5½ (Ref Map 36CSW,1)	
	20th		(2) D horses of Brigade Headquarters took fright, bolted, and were run over by a train.	
	21st	9am- 6am.	Minor operation carried out by C/235th Bty. 1 section of Bty went into action in the open and engaged enemy's support lines.	
	22nd	6am 4.15pm	Similar operation carried out by C/238 c do by C/235th Bty or 21st X/47 T.M. Bty. fired on man & mined wounded a Barrow fleet at M.26.a.15.90 (36.C.SW,1.) to prevent occupation by hostile Infantry. Stokes Mortars supported.	
	24th	8.30- 9.30pm	6 T.M. Batteries fired on hostile wire. Covering fire by a/235, b/235, C/235 and C/238 at the rate of 10 rds per hour	

WAR DIARY
or
INTELLIGENCE SUMMARY.
(Erase heading not required.)

Army Form C. 2118.

Place	Date	Hour	Summary of Events and Information	Remarks and references to Appendices
	26th		Group personnel with the exception of the C.O. and adjutant, O=8 of batteries and a few O.R's were relieved by Officers and O.R's of 315t and 317th Batts. (R.N.D.A.) 238th Bde. moved to SACHIN (R/of Hqrs LENS/M.) Bivouac and transport lines completed.	
	28th		Registration carried out in S. of ANGRES sector.	
		1.30am	Enemy's support trenches engaged by batteries of group for the periods of 4 mins, the operation arranged for protection of officers and O.R. of 1 RNDA.	
	29th	2.45am	Operation of 28th again carried out for the period of 4 mins. Remainder of Personnel of 47th D.A. relieved by 63rd R.N. Div. Arty. Details of 238th Bde. rejoin Brigade at SACHIN	
	30th		Brigade moved to CONCHY-SUR-CANCHE arriving at 4 a.m.	
	31st		resting.	

R.S.Eley
LT. COLONEL R.F.
COMMANDING 238TH BRIGADE R.F.

47th Divisional Artillery.

238th BRIGADE

ROYAL FIELD ARTILLERY.

AUGUST 1916

Army Form C. 2118.

238th Brigade R.F.A. August 1916   47 pars

WAR DIARY
or
INTELLIGENCE SUMMARY.
(Erase heading not required.)

SECRET.

Instructions regarding War Diaries and Intelligence Summaries are contained in F.S. Regs., Part II. and the Staff Manual respectively. Title pages will be prepared in manuscript.

Place	Date AUG.	Hour	Summary of Events and Information	Remarks and references to Appendices
CONCHY-SUR-CANCHE.	1st.		Brigade moved to OUTREBOIS.	
OUTREBOIS.	3rd.		4 L.D. horses received from 47th. D.A.C.	
	5th.		Brigade moved to GENNE-IVERGNAY.	
GENNE-IVERGNY.	6th.		Brigade Headquarters Staff carried out tactical scheme of Signalling.	
	7th.		Brigade carried out tactical scheme. Object of the scheme being practice in taking up "half-cocked" positions, engaging moving troops, communications, and supply of ammunition from parks upwards. The Brigade took up position in observation as Artillery of the rear guard near SELLANDRE.	
	9th.		Brigade carried out a tactical scheme.	
LANCHES	10th.		Brigade moved from Genne-IVERGNY to LANCHES.	
WARGNIES.	11th.		Brigade moved to WARGNIES.	
BAVELINCOURT.	12th.		Brigade moved to BAVELINCOURT. Received 8 remounts from D.A.C.	
	13th.		One Section of each Battery (Less C/238 Bty.) moved up into action at S.20.a. (Ref.Map LONGUEVAL,2b, 1/10,000).	
	14th.		Remaining Sections (Less C/238 Bty.) and Headquarters, moved up into action, relieving 102 Bde., 23rd Div. D/238 Battery carried out a bombardment programme on Road in rear of enemy front line. Headquarters established at X.29.d.9.7. (ref. Map 57D.S.E.,4).	
	15th.		From 8.30 p.m. to 5 a.m. tasks were allotted to Batteries on enemy's frony line communication trenches and Road tracks. Hostile Artillery active during the day on MAMETZ WOOD and BAZENTIN-LE-PETIT WOOD. Ammunition expended to 12 noon - 512 rounds.	
	16th.		Batteries practice barrage on enemy SWITCH LINE from S.2.a.9.3. to S.2.c.½.9. at 4 p.m. From 5 p.m. to 8 p.m. batteries fired on above zone at varying rates of fire. Ammunition expended to 12 noon - 1570 rds. 1 O.R. of D/238 Battery wounded by premature. 34th Battery sent one Gun to I.O.M. with flange of inner spring case stripped.	

T2134. Wt. W708—776. 500000. 4/15. Sr.J.C.&S.

Army Form C. 2118.

WAR DIARY
or
INTELLIGENCE SUMMARY.
(Erase heading not required.)

Instructions regarding War Diaries and Intelligence Summaries are contained in F. S. Regs., Part II. and the Staff Manual respectively. Title pages will be prepared in manuscript.

Place	Date AUG	Hour	Summary of Events and Information	Remarks and references to Appendices
X.29.d.9.7.	17th.		At 8.55 a.m. Batteries barraged their zones 20 yds. short. Enemy plane observed to fall in flames to N.W. of OVILLERS-LA-BOISELLE. Infantry attacked the SWITCH LINE, and throughout the day successfully captured portions of it. Heavy Artillery fire by enemy. Batteries fired continuously throughout day and night. Capt. SWINTON, B/238 Battery, Wounded. Ammunition expended to 12 noon - 1,429 rounds. 1 O.R. of D/238 Battery killed.	
	18th.		Further barraging of SWITCH LINE in S.1. and 2. (Ref. Map LONGUEVAL, 1/10,000.). 15th. Div. Infantry attacked under cover of Smoke Cloud and succeeded in capturing a portion of the line. XXXXXX Enemy heavily barraged our Front and Support Trenches. One gun of B/238 Battery out of action with broken spring, and another sent to I.O.M., both replaced by guns of C/238 Battery. Ammunition expended to 12 noon - 4,750 rounds.	
	19th.		New defensive zones allotted by 47th. Div. Arty. occasioned by our capture of the SWITCH LINE. Barrage of line 200 yards N. of SWITCH LINE carried out, and Roads and Tracks leading from S.W. of MARTINPUICH searched. Ammunition expended to 12 noon - 1,687 rounds.	
	20th.		C/238 Battery relieved B/238 Battery. Enemy intermittently bombarded Battery positions with Gas Shells of small calibre. Ammunition expended to 12 noon - 555 rounds. 2 O.R.S. of C/238 Bty. slightly gassed.	
	21st.		Batteries assisted 50th Division attack by Artillery fire. Battery positions bombarded with Gas Shells. Ammunition expended to 12 noon - 237 rounds. 17 horses received from 236th and 237th Brigades R.F.A.	
	22 - 25th.		Enemy Artillery very active during this period. Our Artillery fired according to programme.	
	22nd.		Ammunition expended to 12 noon - 1,192 rounds.	
	23rd.		Ammunition expended to 12 noon - 268 rounds.	
	24th.		Ammunition expended to 12 noon - 2,578 rounds. 34th Battery sent one gun to I.O.M. (Out of action).	
	25th.		Ammunition expended to 12 noon - 1,055 rounds. 1 O.R. 34th Battery killed and 1 O.R. of Headquarters severely wounded.	
	26th.		Battery positions persistently shelled. 1 Gun of 34th Battery hit and sent to I.O.M. Ammunition expended to 12 noon - 495 rounds.	

Army Form C. 2118.

WAR DIARY
or
INTELLIGENCE SUMMARY.
(*Erase heading not required.*)

Instructions regarding War Diaries and Intelligence Summaries are contained in F.S. Regs., Part II. and the Staff Manual respectively. Title pages will be prepared in manuscript.

Place	Date AUG.	Hour	Summary of Events and Information	Remarks and references to Appendices
X.29.d.9.7.	27th.		Continued activity of Artillery on both sides. Enemy aeroplanes more active. B/238th Battery relieved 34th Battery. Ammunition expended to 12 noon - 60 rounds.	
	28-31st.		Batteries fired according to programme. Hostile artillery active.	
	28th.		Ammunition expended to 12 noon: - 790 rounds. 1 O.R. of B/238 Battery severely wounded. Capt. R.K.Cotter to Fld. Amb. - Sick.	
	29th.		Ammunition expended to 12 noon - 244 rounds. 1 O.R. B/238 Battery wounded from premature by a neighbouring battery.	
	30th.		Ammunition expended to 12 noon - 1,804 rounds.	
	31st.		Ammunition expended to 12 noon - 581 rounds. 1 O.R. B/238 Battery wounded.	

Lt. Colonel R.F.A.
COMMANDING 238TH BRIGADE R.F.A.

SECRET.

WAR DIARY
or
INTELLIGENCE SUMMARY.
(Erase heading not required.)

235th (Howitzer) Brigade R.F.A.

September 1916

Army Form C. 2118.

Place	Date	Hour	Summary of Events and Information	Remarks and references to Appendices
X.29.d.9.7. (Ref.Map 57d.S.E.4.	Sept 1.	Communication	Less enemy artillery activity. Batteries carried out fire on the SWITCH LINE. From 10 p.m. to 4.30 a.m. about 2,000 gas shells fell around Battery positions. 2 guns of C/238 battery were hit. Communication between Brigade Headquarters and Batteries continually broken. 1 O.R. killed and 5 wounded (4 gassed). 56 Horses of "B" battery were gassed. Ammunition expended to 12 noon – 928 rds.	
	2nd		Preliminary bombardment from 2 p.m. to 2.30 p.m. Batteries of Brigade fired on enemy trenches in S.3.a.0.8. to S.2.b.0.8. and then resumed continuous barrage on enemy front linr trenches. 2 O.R.'s wounded (gassed). Ammunition expended to 12 noon – 3,387 rounds.	
	3.		IVth Army attacked in conjunction with the French. XVth Corps attacked GINCHY, and 1st. Division WOOD LANE and enemy front line in HIGH WOOD. 47th D.A. carried out bombardment of enemy front line to assist. Personnel of 34th Battery relieved personnel of "D" Battery in action. Ammunition expended to 12 noon 4,007 rounds.	
	4.		Continuous barrage of enemy lines. Ammunition expended to 12 noon – 3,206 rounds.	
	5.		Continuous barrage of enemy lines. Ammunition expended to 12 noon – 2,451 rounds.	
	6.		Continuous barrage of enemy lines. Capt. Vivian Nickalls posted to 238th Brigade R.F.A. Ammunition expended to 12 noon – 2,439 rounds.	
	7.		Enemy artillery showed more activity as also did their aeroplanes. 1 O.R. killed and 2 O.R.s. wounded. Ammunition expended to 12 noon – 3,566 rounds.	
	8.		1st Division attacked HIGH WOOD. Brigade assisted with Artillery fire – Howitzer Battery on ground N.W. of HIGH WOOD. Bombardment commenced at noon and Infantry attacked at 6 p.m. At 7.30 p.m. 18 Pdrs were taken out of pits to sweep round on enemy at about M.33. Central apparently massing for a counter attack. "D" Battery had a premature and 1 O.R. was wounded. Ammunition expended to 12 noon – 3351 rounds.	
	9.		IVth Army renewed attack. 1st. Div. attacked enemy front line trench from R.35.d.0.3. to R.36.c.5.½. A mine was exploded at S.4.d.2.6½. at 4.45 p.m. A 3 minutes bombardment followed. Attack successful. Continuous barrages maintained. Ammunition expended to 12 noon – 4479 rounds.	

Army Form C. 2118.

SECRET.

WAR DIARY
or
INTELLIGENCE SUMMARY.
(Erase heading not required.)

Instructions regarding War Diaries and Intelligence Summaries are contained in F. S. Regs., Part II. and the Staff Manual respectively. Title pages will be prepared in manuscript.

Place	Date	Hour	Summary of Events and Information	Remarks and references to Appendices
	Sept. 10		Continuous barrages maintained. Brigade attached to 50th Div. Arty. from 5 a.m. 2 O.R.'s. wounded Ammunition expended to 12 noon - 4891 rounds.	
	11.		Continuous barrages maintained. Personnel "B" Battery relieved personnel "C" Battery action. Ammunition expended to 12 noon - 1690 rounds.	
	12.		Brigade rejoined 47th D.A. from 12 noon and took on new front from EAUCOURT L'ABBAYE to FLERS. Ammunition expended to 12 noon - 1478 rounds.	
	13.		Bombardment of enemy lines continued. "D" Battery had a premature from which 1 O.R. was wounded. 2 O.R's. wounded. Ammunition expended to 12 noon - 2,120 rounds.	
	14.		Bombardment continued. 1 Officer and 5 O.R's. wounded. Ammunition expended to 12 noon - 2627 rounds.	
	15.		IVth Army attacked enemy's defences between COMBLES and MARTINPUICH. New Zealand attacked on right and 50th Div. on left. 47th Div. objective to take HIGH WOOD. Batteries of 238th Brigade bombarded trenches in M.34 and Cuttings in S.4. and S.3. Attack partially successful, HIGH WOOD, MARTINPUICH, COURCELETTE and FLERS being taken. Ammunition expended to 12 noon - 5,382 rounds.	
	16.		Further bombardment and attack. 47th Division attacked ridge M.29.b.5.3. to M.34.Central. 238th Brigade bombarded COUGH DROP Dug Outs with all guns and howitzers. Ammunition expended to 12 noon - 6846 rounds.	
	17th		Brigade in Reserve - handing over guns to 235th and 236th Brigades. German counter attack in region of MARTINPUICH successfully repulsed. Lieut. & Adjutant E.R.Cooper temporarily attached to 47th Div. Arty. Ammunition expended to 12 noon - 360 rounds.	
	18-22nd.		Brigade in reserve during this period. Guns and sights being handed over to other Brigades in action, whilst damaged guns were collected and taken to I.O.M. Guns were also collected from I.O.M. and Railhead. Throughout this period Liaison Officers were detailed for duty with Infantry Brigade Headquarters. F.O.O's. were also detailed by Batteries to keep in touch with Infantry and report all matters of general interest and tactical importance.	

SECRET.

WAR DIARY
or
INTELLIGENCE SUMMARY.
(Erase heading not required.)

Army Form C. 2118.

Place	Date	Hour	Summary of Events and Information	Remarks and references to Appendices
S.21.a.1.1.	23rd.		238th. Brigade (Less D/238 Battery) relieved 237th Brigade in action. Bde. Hqrs at S.21.a.1.1. 34th Battery and One Section of "C" Battery relieved A/237 Battery at S.10.a.6.4. "B" Battery and One Section of "C" Battery relieved C/237 Battery at S.10.a.8.6. Wagon lines removed to S. "D" Battery remained in old position and were attached to 237th Brigade.	
	24th		Slow fire maintained on FLERS LINE from M.29.a.9.5. to M.23.c.6.2. from 10.10 p.m. to 12.35 a.m. Lieut. & Adjutant E.R. Cooper returned to Brigade Headquarters.	
	25th.		IVth Army renewed offensive, resulting in the capture of THIEPVAL, GUEDECOURT, LESBOEUFS, MORVAL, and COMBLES. Ammunition expended to 12 noon 1900 rounds.	
	26th.		Canadian Corps attacked at 12.35 p.m. 47th. D.A. assisting with Artillery fire. D/238 Battery relieved D/255 Battery in action at S.9.b.8.2. Ammunition expended to 12 noon - 717 rounds.	
	27th.		Ammunition expended to 12 noon 1365 rounds.	
	28th.		B.G.R.A. requests that FLERS VALLEY be reconnoitred for a gun position to enfilade FLERS TRENCH towards EAUCOURT L'ABBAYE. Batteries fired on FLERS LINE from M.29.a.9.9. to M.23.c.4.3. the enemy being observed there. Enemy observed advancing in open order in M.5.b.c.d. batteries engaged them whilst advancing along Sunken Road in M.11.a. Casualties inflicted and enemy dispersed. D/238 Battery had a premature - 1 O.R. killed and 3 wounded. Ammunition expended to 12 noon - XXXX rds. 2759	
	29th		Barraged FLERS and SUPPORT LINES. 2 O.R's wounded. Ammunition expended to 12 noon - 1298 rds.	
	30th.		Barraged on FLERS and SUPPORT LINES at request of Infantry who were attacking a portion of that line. Ammunition expended to 12 noon - 687 rounds.	

Army Form C. 2118.

SECRET

238 Bde RFA

WAR DIARY
or
INTELLIGENCE SUMMARY.
(Erase heading not required.)

Instructions regarding War Diaries and Intelligence Summaries are contained in F. S. Regs., Part II. and the Staff Manual respectively. Title pages will be prepared in manuscript.

Place	Date	Hour	Summary of Events and Information	Remarks and references to Appendices
S.21.a.1.1. (Ref. Map. 57c.S.W. 1/20,000).	Oct. 1.		Fourth Army renewed attack. The objective of the 47th Division was EAUCOURT L'ABBAYE. Batteries fired on FLERS FRONT and SUPPORT LINES and on the EAUCOURT L'ABBAYE defences. Batteries carried on night firing on road from M.16.b.8.0. to M.16.b.9.8. Ammunition expended to 12 noon - 3,361 rounds. 1 O.R. wounded.	
	2.		Batteries kept up a continuous barrage on M.25.b.0.9. to M.16.d.7.1. Situation as result of previous days attack reported as uncertain. Ammunition expended to 12 noon - 2842 rounds.	
	3.		The O.C. reconnoitred a position with a view to placing a Battery of 6 guns forward to S.5.c. for the purpose of cutting wire in front of the WARLENCOURT LINE. EAUCOURT L'ABBAYE reported as in our hands at 5 p.m. One section of 34th Battery moved forward to new position at S.5.c.6.4. Ammunition expended to 12 noon 363 rounds.	
	4.		Remaining Section of 34th Battery moved up to S.5.c.6.4. WARLENCOURT LINE registered by aeroplane. Night firing carried out on G IRD LINE and new enemy trench running from M.18.c.4.3. to M.17.d.5.5. Ammunition expended to 12 noon - 238 rounds.	
	5.		Batteries fired on German working parties. Further registration of WARLENCOURT LINE by aeroplane. Night firing on Road from M.16.b.8.0. to M.16.b.9.9. Infantry successfully attacked and took the MILL in M.22.b. Ammunition expended to 12 noon - 1025 rounds.	
	6.		Batteries carried out, from 3.15 p.m. to 5.15 p.m., a bombardment of WARLENCOURT LINE from M.17.b.0.5. to M.18.c.0.9½. and GIRD TRENCH from M.18.c.0.9½. to M.17.b.5.3. Ammunition expended to 12 noon - 1266 rds.	
	7.		Fourth Army resumed offensive. The objective of the 47th Division was the BUTTE DE WARLENCOURT to M.18.a.1.3. Batteries formed a creeping barrage throughout this attack. Night firing carried out on objectives. Ammunition expended to 12 noon - 877 rounds.	
	8.		Batteries ceased firing on objectives of yesterday at 10 a.m. Registration carried out of line from M.17.d.7.4. to M.17.d.0.5. and road from M.22.b.4.8. to M.16.d.6½.3. Night firing on GIRD FRONT LINE from BUTTE DE WARLENCOURT to M.17.b.5.3. As a result of yesterday's attack 8 officers and 478 O.R.s. were taken prisoners. Ammunition expended to 12 noon - 4,375 rounds.	
	9.		Battery Wagon Lines moved to vicinity of Brigade Headquarters. in S.21.a.1.1. Batteries fired on trench from M.17.c.0.3. to M.17.b.4.5. "B" Battery Staff relieved 34th Battery Staff in action.	

T2134. Wt. W708—776. 50C000. 4/15. Str J.C.&S.

Army Form C. 2118.

SECRET

WAR DIARY
or
INTELLIGENCE SUMMARY.

(Erase heading not required.)

Instructions regarding War Diaries and Intelligence Summaries are contained in F. S. Regs., Part II. and the Staff Manual respectively. Title pages will be prepared in manuscript.

Place	Date	Hour	Summary of Events and Information	Remarks and references to Appendices
	9.	(Contd)	Batteries carried out night firing. Searchlight in use by enemy at M.17.d. Ammunition expended to 12 noon - 1081 rounds.	
	10.		Major General GORRINGE, G.O.C. 47th Division, with C.O. visited Batteries. "D" Battery fired on new trench from M.17.d.3.5. to M.17.a.8.4½ from 10 p.m. to 12 midnight, and again from 4 a.m. to 6 a.m. Ammunition expended to 12 noon - 1189 rounds.	
	11.		Batteries barraged from M.18.c.1.4½. to M.17.d.7.4½. Night firing carried out on line from M.17.b.0.5. to M.18.a.0.0. Officers of 51st and 52nd Brigades, 9th Division, attached to Batteries. Ammunition expended to 12 noon - 280 rounds.	
	12.		Fourth Army renewed attack. Objective of 9th Division was the German line in M.17.c.d. Batteries maintained a creeping barrage during this attack. Night firing carried out on line from M.17.a.8.6. to M.10.b.9.2. Gun and carriage of "B" Battery sent to I.O.M. Ammunition expended to 12 noon - 1679 rds. 14 remounts received.	
	13.		Ammunition expended to 12 noon - 3422 rounds. Brigade relieved in action by 52nd Brigade, 9th Division, and marched to bivouacs at E AVELINCOURT.	
BAVELIN-COURT. (AMIENS F.1.)	14.		Brigade at rest.	
	15.		Brigade marched to TALMAS.	
TALMAS (LENS 11 D.6.).	16.		Brigade marched to AUTHIEULE.	
AUTHIEULE (LENS, E 5).	17.		Brigade marched to CONCHY-SUR-CANCHE.	
CONCHY-SUR-CANCHE. (LENS.C.3)	18.		Continued march to FONTAINE-LES-BOULANS.	
FONTAINE-LES-BOULANS (LENS D.1.)	19.		Continued march to MAMETZ.	

Army Form C. 2118.

SECRET

WAR DIARY
or
INTELLIGENCE SUMMARY.
(Erase heading not required.)

Instructions regarding War Diaries and Intelligence Summaries are contained in F. S. Regs, Part II. and the Staff Manual respectively. Title pages will be prepared in manuscript.

Place	Date	Hour	Summary of Events and Information	Remarks and references to Appendices
MAMETZ (HAZEBROUCK 5a,D.5.).	20.		Continued march to WATOU.	
WATOU (HAZEBROUCK 5a,H.2.).	21.		One Section of each battery relieved section of batteries of 2nd Australian Division in action.	
	22.		Brigade Headquarters marched to G.23.c.5.5. Remaining sections of batteries marched into action. Batteries attached as follows for tactical purposes.:- 34th Battery to 235th Brigade, R.F.A., forming RIGHT GROUP. "B" Battery to 236th Brigade, R.F.A., forming LOWE GROUP. "C" Battery to 237th Brigade, R.F.A., forming LEFT GROUP. "D" Battery to 237th Brigade, R.F.A., forming LEFT GROUP.	
	23.		Lt.-Col. E.H. ELEY, C.M.G., O.C., 238th Brigade R.F.A., assumed command of RIGHT GROUP. 19 reinforcements arrived from Base. 8 Telephonists of Brigade Headquarters attached to LOWE GROUP.	
	24.		2/Lt. R.W.MILES, Orderly Officer, 238th Brigade R.F.A., attached LOWE GROUP for duty.	
	25.		2/Lt. J.Falcke and 3 O.Rs. proceeded on leave.	
	30.		Lieut. and Adjutant, E.R.COOPER,M.C., attached to 47th Div. Arty.	
	31.		D.D.V.S., Second Army, inspected horses of Brigade.	

Lieut.-Col., R.F.A.,T.F.,
Commanding,
238th Brigade R.F.A.

WAR DIARY November 1916

INTELLIGENCE SUMMARY.

(Erase heading not required.)

Army Form C. 2118.

238th Bde R.F.A.

SECRET.

Place	Date	Hour	Summary of Events and Information	Remarks and references to Appendices
G.23.c.5.5 (Ref.Map 28,N.W.) 1/20000.	Nov.1916 4th		D.D.R., 2nd Army, inspected fractious horses for the purpose of casting.	
	11th		24 Remounts collected.	
	12th		Lt. and Adjt. E.R.COOPER proceeded on leave.	
	13th		Lt.Col. E.H.ELEY, C.M.G., ceased command of Right Group. 2/Lt. W.B.FOORD-KELCEY, 'B' Battery transferred to 'C' Battery. 2/Lt. D.F.BOYD, 'C' Battery transferred to 'D' Battery. B.S.M.GRACE, 'B' Battery transferred to 'D' Battery. B.S.M. E.W.SALE, 'D' Battery, transferred to 'B' Battery.	
	14th		Lt. Col. E.H.ELEY, C.M.G. proceeded on one month's leave.	
	20th		G.O.C., Division inspected wagon lines.	
	23rd		16 L.D. Remounts collected.	
	25th		1 Officer and 3 O.R's. proceeded on leave.	
	27th		Re-organisation of Artillery B brigades carried out.	
			238th Brigade formed as follows:-	
			34th Battery and one section of 'B' Battery formed new 34th Battery. 'C' " " " " " " 'B' " " " " 'B' Battery. B/237 " " " " " C/237 " " " " 'C' Battery. 'D' Battery remained as before.	
	28th		Divisional Artillery Order placed Lt. Col. W. E. PEAL in command of 238th Brigade, R.F.A.	

Army Form C. 2118.

WAR DIARY
or
INTELLIGENCE SUMMARY.
(Erase heading not required.)

Instructions regarding War Diaries and Intelligence Summaries are contained in F. S. Regs., Part II. and the Staff Manual respectively. Title pages will be prepared in manuscript.

Place	Date	Hour	Summary of Events and Information	Remarks and references to Appendices
	28th		(Contd) during absence on leave of Lt. Col. E. H. ELEY, C.M.G. Lieut and Adjt. E.R.COOPER, M.C., on leave, reported unfit to return, and struck off strength.	

R M Miles Lt
for
Lieut. Col., R.F.A., T.F.,
Commanding
238th Brigade, R.F.A.

SECRET.

Army Form C. 2118.

238 "Bde RFA Vol 22

WAR DIARY
or
INTELLIGENCE SUMMARY.
(Erase heading not required.)

Place	Date	Hour	Summary of Events and Information	Remarks and references to Appendices
G.23.c.5.5. (Ref. Map, 28, N.W. 1/20,000).	1916 DEC.	1-24.	Batteries in action with Left Group, Lt. Col. W.E.Peal commanding :- 34th Battery at I.19.B.1.7 'B' " " I.20.d.0.2. 'C' " B (R. Sec. at I.26.d.½.2. " " (L. Sec. at I.26.b.3.3. 'D' " at I.20.c.7.½. During this period much work was carried out improving the condition and accommodation of the Wagon Lines.	
	1st		Lieut. H. Spencer to England for Gunnery Course.	
	3rd		Presentation of ribbons by Divisional Commander at Halifax Camp.	
	5th		Lieut. Ballantyne posted to 'C' Battery.	
	6th		Capt. L.S.Lloyd proceeded to England and struck off strength.	
	8th		Lieut. H. Carey Morgan to England for Gunnery Course.	
	15th		Lt. Col. E. H. Eley returned from leave.	
	22nd		The following postings were made:- Major N.E.Wood to command 'B' Battery Captain J. Simonds " 34th "	
	24th		Lt. Col. E.H.Eley assumed command of Left Group with Headquarters at Railway Dug-Outs I.21.c.6.8. The position was heavily shelled.	

Army Form C. 2118.

WAR DIARY
or
INTELLIGENCE SUMMARY.
(Erase heading not required.)

Instructions regarding War Diaries and Intelligence Summaries are contained in F. S. Regs., Part II. and the Staff Manual respectively. Title pages will be prepared in manuscript.

Place	Date	Hour	Summary of Events and Information	Remarks and references to Appendices
I.21.c.6.8.1916 (Ref.Map, 28 N.W. 1/20,000)	DEC. 26th		34th Battery received one section from Lowe's Group.	
	27th		Batteries fired.	
			Trench Mortars carried out 'shoot' on suspected mine workings at I.29.c.60.15.	
			'C' Battery received their 3rd Section from Lowe's Group.	
	28th		Lieut. R.B.Ullman posted to 'C' Battery from this date.	
			Aeroplane registration carried out by O/236 Battery.	
	29th		Capt. Jacoby reported to A/235 Battery.	

E.H.Rier(?)

Lieut. Col. R.F.A., T.F.
Commanding
238th Brigade R.F.A.

238 Bde RFA.
(late:—
8 London (How) Bde)

January 1917.

Index..........

SUBJECT.

No.	Contents.	Date.

The 2ⁿᵈ Division (V Corps)

in the

Battle of the Ancre,

13 - 17/XI/1916

Compiled by

Lt. E. Wyrall,

Historian 2ⁿᵈ Division

Dec. 1920/Jan. 1921.)

FILE 7.

HISTORICAL SECTION
MILITARY BRANCH.

1915 (VOL.1)

YPRES, 1915

Sketch 12 _ Battle of St Julien, 24th April

(Corrected 1st Proof)

Instructions enclosed

238 Bde R.F.A.
147 Div Arty Gp
SECRET.
Vol 323

Army Form C. 2118.

WAR DIARY
or
INTELLIGENCE SUMMARY.
(Erase heading not required.)

Instructions regarding War Diaries and Intelligence Summaries are contained in F.S. Regs., Part II. and the Staff Manual respectively. Title pages will be prepared in manuscript.

Place	Date	Hour	Summary of Events and Information	Remarks and references to Appendices
I.21.c.6.8 (Ref. Map, 28, N.W.3, 1/20,000)	1917. JAN. 1st.	6.10 p.m.	Heavy bombardment by enemy on left of Group Front. Infantry sent up S.O.S. Signal there, at 6.10 p.m. Batteries of Group formed a barrage. At 6.30 p.m. ceased firing.	
	3rd.		2/Lieut. R.W.MILES, on return from leave, took over Adjutant's duties. Wirecutting carried out by B/238 Battery.	
	4th.		C/236 Battery carried out wire-cutting. C/236 Battery registered enemy's trench system from I.35.a.4.6 to I.35.a.60.75 as detailed for forthcoming bombardment. Group Commander reconnoitred re-inforcement positions as in Scheme 'X'.	
	5th.		Wirecutting carried out by B/238 Battery at I.35.a.5.7. From 2.30 p.m. to 3.30 p.m. and 3.45 p.m. to 4.15 p.m. Heavy Artillery and 4.5" Hows. carried out a bombardment of enemy's trench system. 18 pdrs. and Trench Mortar Batteries cooperated.	
	6th.		C/238 Battery position heavily shelled during whole morning with 200 4.2.s and 100 5.9.s. One gun-pit was hit but no damage was done.	
	7th.		Group Commander observed and reported to D.A. on wire-cutting carried out by B/238 Battery at I.35.a.50.65. C/238 Battery cut wire at I.29.d.5.5.	
	8th.		Group Commander lectured at Divisional School, POPERINGHE.	
	9th.		New Retaliation Scheme 'L' came into force.	
	10th.		C/238 Battery registered lone gun. 34th Battery heavily shelled from 1 p.m. to 2.45 p.m. 1 O.R. killed.	
	11th.		Batteries fired in retaliation for minenwerfer activity by the enemy.	
	12th.		Corps C.R.A. and B.G., R.A., visited batteries of the Group. At 3.40 p.m. and again at 9.10 p.m. batteries fired in retaliation for hostile shelling of our trenches.	

Army Form C. 2118.

SECRET.

WAR DIARY
or
INTELLIGENCE SUMMARY.
(Erase heading not required.)

Instructions regarding War Diaries and Intelligence Summaries are contained in F.S. Regs., Part II. and the Staff Manual respectively. Title pages will be prepared in manuscript.

Place	Date	Hour	Summary of Events and Information	Remarks and references to Appendices
	1916. JAN 1916			
	15th.		At 4 p.m. batteries carried out retaliation for enemy shelling RAILWAY CUTTING in I.29.C. Major Lord GORELL, O.C., C/238 Battery, wounded near LARCH WOOD.	
	16th.		Major Lord GORELL died of wounds. Batteries of Group bombarded enemy front and support trenches in accordance with 47th D.A. Operation Order No. 1. Retaliation carried out by batteries from Scheme 'L' for heavy hostile shelling of RAILWAY CUTTING and Left Battalion Headquarters.	
	17th.		B/238 and C/236 Batteries fired on road through I.36.b. from 10 p.m. to 11 p.m. and from 1.0 a.m. to 2.0 a.m.	
	18th.		Commanding Officer attended inspection of Wagon Lines by Army Commander.	
	19th.		Major. N.E.WOOD, O.C. B/238 Battery, posted to command C/238 Battery. Capt. H.JACOBY, B/235 Battery, transferred to B/238 Battery.	
	20th. to 21st.		Brigade ceased to exist. B/238 Battery transferred to 189th Brigade, R.F.A. C/238 Battery became C/104 Battery. C/238 Battery became C/236 Battery. D/238 Battery became D/235 Battery. Lt.Col. E.H.ELEY, C.M.G., handed over command of LEFT GROUP to Lt.Col. LOWE, 236th Brigade, R.F.A.	

EH Eley

Lieut.Col., R.F.A., T.F.,
Commanding,
238th Brigade, R.F.A.

www.ingramcontent.com/pod-product-compliance
Lightning Source LLC
Chambersburg PA
CBHW081535160426
43191CB00011B/1767